The Old Testament Understanding of God

The Old Testament
Understanding
of God

by

J. Stanley Chesnut

The Westminster Press
Philadelphia

LIBRARY OF CONGRESS CATALOG CARD NO. 68–10436

PUBLISHED BY THE WESTMINSTER PRESS ®
PHILADELPHIA, PENNSYLVANIA
PRINTED IN THE UNITED STATES OF AMERICA

To my parents
Atwood W. and Lillian Chesnut
in gratitude and affection

Contents

Preface	9
Introduction	13
I. God in Early Hebrew Thought	27
II. The God of Moses	44
III. The Lord of Hosts: God and War	59
IV. God and Kingship	70
V. God in the Early Prophetic View	82
VI. The Great Prophets Speak for God	95
VII. God in the Later Prophetic View	113
VIII. God and the Religion of Israel	129
IX. God in Wisdom and Poetry	147
X. God of the Covenant: Old and New	165
Selected Bibliography	176
Notes	179
Index	187

Contents

Preface
Introduction

Preface

This book is about the ideas of God in the Old Testament. It attempts to discover the most significant expressions of ancient Israel's understanding of God, who was known to her as Yahweh, and to relate these expressions to the ongoing history of Israel's religion. The emphasis in this book upon the fact of God's existence, coming at a time when the so-called "death of God" theology has attracted an unusual amount of attention, does *not* represent a response to the challenge of that theology. The existence of God is an assumed fundamental of Old Testament thought, and the recognition of that assumption is a first step toward understanding the Old Testament.

It is hoped that a book such as this will be useful to those general readers, of whatever faith or of none, who are interested in a brief, comprehensive survey of Hebrew thought about God as represented by the Old Testament. Readers who stand within the Christian tradition may be especially interested in what the Old Testament has to say about God and in the relationship of these ideas to New Testament thought. For students, the book seeks to provide the kind of information and insight that will add to their learning experience, and for teachers, in both religious and secular institutions, these pages offer a nontechnical treatment of one of the most important subjects of religious knowledge and education.

A great deal of work has been done in the field of Old Testament study in recent decades, and several important books on Old Testament theology have appeared. As a survey of the Old

Testament understanding of God this book presents some of the results of this research, but its purpose is not simply to summarize the contributions of scholarship to the study of the Old Testament. Despite the obvious perils involved, the author's own views have more often than not tended to dominate his use of the work of others. For this and for other reasons, the notes have been kept to a minimum and are largely explanatory in nature. The Selected Bibliography will indicate some of the sources used and will suggest additional reading for the interested student.

In a book of this length it is not possible to include all the ideas relating to God throughout the Old Testament. It was necessary to be selective, while attempting to discuss as many of the major concepts about God as possible. The arrangement of the chapters is basically topical-chronological, insofar as this can be done at all, for many ideas do not fit neatly into a single time period. The topics selected are representative of Old Testament thought about God, providing a carefully chosen framework within which the Old Testament understanding of God may be meaningfully studied.

Finally, but by no means least in importance, this book seeks above all to hear and to convey what the Old Testament itself has to say. To this end it can serve only as a guide to the thought and content of the Old Testament, the full significance of which the reader must always discover for himself. Any success that the book may have in this regard can be measured only by the degree to which it faithfully represents the essential self-understanding of the Old Testament writers.

It is a pleasure to express here my appreciation to those who have contributed in one way or another to my learning and thinking over the past twenty years. My study of the Bible began at the University of Tulsa with Profs. R. Grady Snuggs, Eugene S. Tanner, and the late Walter E. Stuermann. My interest in Old Testament study was kindled at McCormick Theological Seminary by Profs. Ovid R. Sellers, G. Ernest Wright, and Frank M. Cross, Jr., and was nourished at Yale University by Profs. Millar Burrows, B. Davie Napier, and Marvin Pope. To all of these scholars and teachers, and to numerous colleagues and students, I am grateful for whatever I have come to know and understand about the Old Testament. None of them are, of course, responsible in any way for the imperfections of this book.

My thanks go also to Mrs. Stewart Brown for her efficient and prompt typing of the manuscript in its final form. And to my wife, Vlasta, and my children, who have endured with patience and understanding the times when "writing the book" interfered with normal family routine, I offer my greatest appreciation for their considerable contribution to my life and work.

J. S. C.

Introduction

God is at the center of Old Testament religious thought—with this assertion there will be little argument. Students of the Bible have always recognized that an adequate understanding of both the Old and New Testaments must begin with and always return to the fact of God. A variety of interpretative themes—election, covenant, creation, history, redemption—have proved to be of value in the study of Scripture, but their value depends entirely upon the degree to which they heighten our awareness of the centrality of God.

Almost every page of the Old Testament reveals this consciousness of the presence of God. He is there as the One who brought all things into being and who makes all things possible. At times he is present with his people in intimate and uplifting fellowship; at other times he presents his will in unyielding aloofness and power. It is God who determines the course of human events, whether in the immediate affairs of an individual, the vicissitudes of national history, or the sudden catastrophe that overthrows a mighty empire. And it is God who sees the needs of his people, who provides and sustains, who chastises and comforts, who moves through the long corridors of time to save, to redeem, and to restore.

In the Old Testament, affirmations such as these are the product of a response to *events*. Instead of working out logically or systematically a concept of God that would satisfy their intellectual and spiritual needs, the people of the Old Testament, for whatever psychological or sociological reasons, saw the essence of God's being in human history, and in this faith they committed their destiny into his keeping. Theirs was a faith that often questioned and rebelled against his will, but never doubted the fact of his being and his right to exercise authority over his people. This lack of real interest in the question of God's existence is a significant feature of the Old Testament understanding of God.

THE EXISTENCE OF GOD

From the Hebrew point of view, the existence of God is not debatable. He *is,* and the writers of ancient Israel throughout the Old Testament simply assume that he is. The faith of Israel, conditioned and determined as it was in concrete realities, had little reason or room for abstract speculation. The people had encountered God in the everyday experiences of their lives. Abraham met God in the tents of his encampment, in the sun-scorched paths of his journeys, and in the crises that beset his family and kinsmen. Moses was confronted by God not only on the remote and hostile mountaintop, but also in the halls of Pharaoh's palace, in the desperate trek across Sinai, and in the sacred Tent of Meeting. The kings and prophets of Israel believed that God had anointed them with his holy charisma, that he directed the course of national life, and that he spoke his word to them in "many and various ways." And Job was shocked into painful awareness of the presence of God through his experience of suffering, questioning, doubting, and confessing.

It is this experiential awareness of God that is most characteristic of the Old Testament. Since the faith of Israel reveals no theological speculation about the existence of God, we may be tempted to conclude, somewhat smugly, that this is due to Israel's lack of theological sophistication and to her essentially "primitive" religion. Such a conclusion would represent a serious misunderstanding of the nature of Old Testament faith, for the depth of insight and the vitality of religious life in ancient Israel are in no sense lessened by her failure to raise what may seem to us the primary theological question. We would do well to consider the possibility that the debate among theologians and philosophers concerning the existence of God is symptomatic of a decline in religious vitality and in what we may call "practical theism."

Having recognized this premise of the Old Testament—that God *is*—one is still faced with the necessity of inquiring what the Old Testament has to say *about* God. Who he is, what he is, the meaning of his acts, his relationship to his people—these are some of the questions that concerned ancient thinkers as much as they concern contemporary theologians—but the answers to these questions are far from being universally clear in the Old Testament. What can we know about God? This is the question that is everywhere present in the Bible; indeed, it is the question to which the Bible itself is largely an answer.

THE KNOWLEDGE OF GOD

From what has been said above about the nature of Old Testament thought, it is not surprising that we find little conscious epistemology in Old Testament writings. The writers do not concern themselves with discussion of how God is known or ways of knowing God, but in what they write, whether it be history, story, poetry, prophecy, or law, God is always present. They are constantly aware of God and they know about him, but without feeling compelled to analyze their experience of the knowledge of God. In fact, the knowledge of God is conceived in such intimate and personal terms that some Old Testament writers, such as the prophet Hosea, employ the same term for knowledge of God and for human sexual experience.

Among the prophets, there is undoubtedly the greatest consciousness of the manner in which God is known. Many of the earlier spokesmen for God, including Moses, seem to have sought out the divine presence and word, confident that God would speak to them or in some manner make himself known. For the most part, however, the prophets simply accepted the fact that God had chosen to speak to and through them and to reveal his will in the spoken word. Even when the word is felt as "a burning fire shut up in my bones" (Jer. 20:9), the prophet is sure that he has been chosen a divine spokesman. He does not know how or why this is so, only that the "burden of the LORD" is upon him.

Others in the Old Testament seem to share this experience, although not with the same intense awareness of having been separated out to be God's spokesmen. Most of the Old Testament writers, other than the prophets, did not think of what they were writing as "sacred scripture" or even as direct communication from God. In The Psalms and Wisdom Literature, for example, we find primarily a note of hope and trust in God's presence and purposive activity, but not a conviction that the writer's own expression represents the mind of God. The psalmists "seek God's face," all the while knowing that God takes the initiative in making himself known, and that man does not discover more than God chooses to uncover:

> Make me to know thy ways, O LORD;
>   teach me thy paths.
> Lead me in thy truth, and teach me,
>   for thou art the God of my salvation;
>   for thee I wait all the day long.
>   (Ps. 25:4–5.)

The author of The Book of Job seems particularly pessimistic about man's finding out "the deep things of God." Job asserts that man does not know the way to the place of wisdom and understanding, and that only God understands the way to it and knows its place (Job 28:12–13, 23). Job, like every man, is forced to conclude that the mysteries of God are too much for him and that when he attempts to search out these secrets and understand them he simply doesn't know what he is talking about (Job 42:2–3). Throughout the book of Proverbs there runs the theme that the ultimate source of human wisdom is the LORD. For the sages, who were concerned almost entirely with a very pragmatic kind of knowledge, common sense and reason are the keys that unlock the chambers of wisdom. There is little in Proverbs that reflects a consciousness of God making himself known to his people. Ecclesiastes sees, on the one hand, that God gives wisdom, knowledge, and joy to the man who pleases him (Eccl. 2:26), but, on the other hand, that man cannot find out and know "all the work of God" (Eccl. 8:17). In general, Ecclesiastes shares with Job a rather deep pessimism with regard to man's knowing and understanding the nature and purpose of God. This position, representing late Jewish thought, contrasts sharply with the earlier prophetic conviction that God is known directly and fully in vision and the spoken word.

The subject of revelation and its forms is too extensive for treatment in depth and in detail in this introduction. The modes of the divine self-disclosure—history, personal experience, the spoken and written word, nature, and even divination—demand intensive and individual investigation, and the Old Testament provides an abundance of material for such studies. What must be said, however, is that men of faith have always seen in the pages of the Old Testament something of the truth of God. We may not expect to know and understand the fullness of his Being, for we who are mortal must let God be God—this is the doubly profound insight of Gen., ch. 3—in all the categories of his Being, but we can share the conviction of the centuries that the Old Testament word remains a high achievement in the history of man's comprehension of God.

THE IDEA OF HISTORICAL REVELATION

The study of the Old Testament understanding of God has proceeded in a variety of ways in the past, ranging from a thoroughgoing Christological interpretation to a highly rationalistic sociohistorical approach. Unfortunately, no single methodology has proved to be generally acceptable. During recent decades studies in this area have usually followed one of two distinct methods: a systematic treatment of the *history* of Israel's religion or a topical presentation of the religious *thought* of the Old Testament. These two methods are obviously closely interrelated, and there have been attempts to combine them in works on the Old Testament, but ordinarily it is the second method that is meant when one speaks of the study of Old Testament theology.

Theology, in the strictest sense as the study of God, is everywhere present in the Old Testament. But at the same time there is, strictly speaking, no systematic theology in the Old Testament. Post-Biblical dogmatic theology is not to be identified with Biblical theology, although its subject matter is identical with the religious ideas of the Bible in most cases, because dogmatics goes beyond Biblical thought in its use of ideas drawn from human reason and philosophical speculation. The real task of Old Testament theology is to find what the faith of Israel had to say about God, and in doing this the student must become involved in the study of a considerable variety of religious concepts, from the primitivism of some of the earliest traditions to the lofty monotheism of the later prophets. This is not simply a matter of tracing genetically the evolution of a lower religion to a higher form—as in some "history of religion" schools—but is, rather, one that requires the assessment of each level of religious awareness and thought in terms of its own unique characteristics and contributions, as well as of whatever came before and after.

The best way to do this is to start with the acknowledgment that the Old Testament understands God to have revealed himself in and through history. The central proposition here is that Israel's religious life is the product of a historical faith—a faith that God has acted repeatedly in history for his own purposes and for his people. Some scholars have even gone so far as to say that the study of this faith in its creedal expression is the only proper subject of Old Testament theology. While this is too limited a view of the matter, one can certainly agree that Old Testament *theology* should be concerned primarily with God, not with religious institutions and rituals, the nature of worship, systems of ethics, or anything else but the fact of God and his relation to man. In this way the "doctrines" of man, the world, sin, salvation, death and the future life—the traditional topics of Old Testament theology—are not central, but derive their meaning from the understanding of what God is and does.

A final point to be noted about the idea of historical revelation is that it does not depend for its rationale upon the concepts of progress, development, or evolution. For all its various levels of understanding, the Old Testament faith did not simply grow, in the classical anthropological analysis, from animism to polytheism to monotheism in the space of a few centuries. If we set aside our philosophical and theological presuppositions as we approach the study of the Old Testament, it will become evident that Israel's faith diverged radically from that of her contemporaries in the ancient Near East. Although there is much in the Old Testament that derived from earlier cultures, especially from the peoples of Mesopotamia, the development of Israel's religion can be viewed as a kind of mutation in the history of Near Eastern religions. Faith in Yahweh was characterized by several unusual concepts, including the idea of his self-revelation in human history. This idea will thus be an essential key to the Old Testament understanding of God.

The Problem of Unity and Diversity

The variety of religious thought and belief in the Old Testament is only one side of the coin. On the other we find a basic unity that is not at all surprising when we keep in mind the cohesiveness of Israel's historical experience, and especially the prophetic interpretation of that experience. On the surface the Old Testament writings appear extremely complex and diverse. Consider the theological naïveté of the Yahwist tradition in Gen., chs. 2 and 3, against the monotheism of Second Isaiah. Or the reflections of demonism in Gen., ch. 32, and Ex., ch. 4, against the awareness of the presence of God expressed in Ps. 27 and Isa., ch. 6. In terms of literary types alone, the Old Testament is a remarkably inclusive sort of collection: laws, history, lyric poetry, legends, prophecy, chronicles, stories, letters, proverbs, essays, psalms and songs, and several other subtypes.

What is it, then, that lends unity to this unusual anthology? It is basically the belief in God, the One who gives meaning to all things. But beyond that, it is the conviction that God moves in and through the lives of his own people toward the accomplishment of his purpose. The prophetic view of history, which is not confined merely to the prophetic writings but is found in much of the Old Testament, insisted that God is most clearly seen in the meaning of events over which he exercised his unquestioned control. Even those who, like Moses, Gideon, Jonah, or Job, resisted or questioned his purpose were soon brought to acknowledge his sovereignty and his sometimes inscrutable ways.

Thus, despite the diversity of insight and expression in the Old Testament understanding of God, there appears throughout a unifying consciousness of the positive and dynamic relationship between God and his people. Unity in diversity is a familiar theme in Biblical studies, and it is one which still may be profitably utilized as we search for the essential truths of the faith of Israel. And to see more clearly what Israel believed about her God is, at the same time, to approach a fuller comprehension of Christian faith in the object of ultimate concern, for there is a unity that reaches beyond the Old Testament to encompass the New Testament in a whole which demands our response to the authority of both its parts.

THE "LANGUAGE" OF THE OLD TESTAMENT

One of the principal requirements for the study of any literary document is an understanding of the way in which the author uses words. To ask about the sort of language employed by the author is to inquire into the nature of his thought and intention rather than into the manner of his diction or choice of words. The problem of the original language of a document—Hebrew, Greek, Aramaic, or whatever—is not at issue here, except that we must recognize the difficulty of transferring certain ideas from one language to another in translation. What we are concerned with is the attempt to discern in writings such as we have in the Old Testament an author's point of view and purpose. Failure to do this, as we can see so readily in much Biblical interpretation, both past and present, leads inevitably to asking the wrong questions, and thus receiving the wrong answers.

For the Old Testament as a whole, it is not possible to speak of one language, in the sense described above. The student must try to discover for each literary work, and sometimes for different parts of a single work, the special conceptual framework and presuppositions of the writer. The tools of literary analysis, comparison, classification, and evaluation are quite useful here, but they do not alone provide sufficient insight into an author's real purpose. Literary criticism is simply the servant of theological interpretation, and the primary imperative of the latter is to understand that religious truth is always represented by a kind of language which cannot be employed meaningfully to represent the truths of science or other "objective" realms of knowledge. Religious language is essentially poetic, or nonprosaic. It involves symbolism, imagery, hyperbole, metaphor, simile, and other word devices that tend to be emotionally as well as intellectually charged with meaning. It is representational rather than presentational language, for the most part.

What has just been said should in no way be taken to mean that religious language, in the Old Testament especially, is not in touch with reality. We can never escape the fact that Biblical language is grounded in history and that its categories and terminology are derived from belief in a God who is known first of all in historical events. But it is the *interpretation* of these events in terms of theological insight that must be emphasized. All the literature of the Bible is "sacred" because it cannot be understood in a secular manner. It must be read as religious literature because that is how it was written, regardless of the particular type involved, whether it is law, legend, narrative, or proverb. When we look at an account such as the Creation story in Gen., ch. 1, we should see immediately that the author was not really interested in describing *how* the world was created; he was interested in *why* it was created and, above all, in *who* created it. What we learn from this account is that the world was created because of the love and goodness of God, who is Creator and Lord of all. This is clearly an example of the use of religious language, and to ask scientific questions of this kind of literature is really nonsensical.

The term "myth" has been used to describe such religious literature in the Old Testament, and it is an appropriate term when rightly understood. When we speak of myth in Genesis, or elsewhere in the Bible for that matter, we do not mean something that is fabricated from fantasy, some form of fiction intended purely for entertainment. Myth refers to a way of expressing the most profound insights and truths of man's religious consciousness, a representation in words of what man understands and believes. Myth employs the kind of religious language we have been describing, and as such is an extremely important category of religious thought. It should never be used to refer to literature or thought that is considered to be inferior or valueless just because it uses this special kind of language.

We may conclude from this discussion that the language of the Old Testament used in speaking about God will be symbolic, representational, mythopoeic, religious language. It may also be described as anthropomorphic, representing the nature and person of God in manlike terms (see below, Ch. I). Theologians will always be hard pressed to find any other way of talking about God. A great many problems in the study of the Bible will be eliminated by beginning with this understanding of the language of the Bible.

DEMYTHOLOGIZING THE OLD TESTAMENT

Something must be said at this point about one of the most challenging insights to have come from twentieth-century Biblical studies. Rudolf Bultmann, the influential German scholar, is generally credited with the suggestion that since the mythological world view of the Bible is no longer acceptable to modern thought, it must therefore be "demythologized." His concern was to present the meaning of the Bible in such a way that it may provide a truly relevant understanding of man's life here and now.

The problem that Bultmann and others saw in the message of the Bible, beginning with the New Testament, was that its language went beyond the merely historical to express a faith in the *meaning* of history. In so doing, the writers of the Bible used mythological ideas and expressions that now must be "translated" for a scientific age. Our view of the cosmos has little in common with that of Biblical man, and thus we find it virtually impossible to think as he did in terms of a literal heaven and hell, divine intervention in history, demon possession, incarnation, resurrection, ascension, and similar concepts.

By demythologizing the Biblical message is meant the processs of cutting away this mythological language until one arrives at the genuinely historical core, while at the same time recognizing that the purpose of Biblical language was to express the real meaning and significance of the historical events. In the case of the Old Testament this would mean giving up the allegorical interpretation of narratives and other material, the literalistic understanding of many "historical" accounts, and the insistence that the truth value of Biblical statements depends primarily upon their historicity. Carried to its extreme, this method makes it virtually impossible to find any acceptable symbolic use of language in the Scriptures. The search must always be for an immediate and personal relevance in the message of the Bible, for light upon the meaning of human existence at this particular moment. Thus the idea that the Old Testament may be translated symbolically and the reduction of the Old Testament material to the "merely historical" are both rejected as inappropriate to such an existentialistic understanding.

The demythologizing school of thought obviously says some things that have needed saying, both to the church and to the world. The element of personal involvement in what has too often been thought of as the dead past, in regard to both the Old and New Testaments, is a valuable and necessary emphasis for a life of faith. Moreover, it has long been recognized in scholarly circles that the message of the Bible, and consequently the message of the church, must be translated into meaningful terms for the times in which we live. The question whether this can best be done through representational or through presentational language, i.e., in a symbolic or in a nonsymbolic way, has not been settled. It is with this problem that students of the Bible will be increasingly concerned in the immediate future, stimulated in large measure by suggestions derived from the program of demythologizing.

The Old Testament God in Christian Faith

For the vast majority of Christians, there has never been any serious difficulty in identifying the Old Testament God with "the God and Father of our Lord Jesus Christ." The rather striking differences at certain points between the Old Testament view of God and the understanding of God in the pages of the New Testament have been accepted as due primarily to the changing conceptions of the Hebrew and Christian communities as God's will was more and more made clear to his people. The God of Abraham, Isaac, and Jacob simply revealed himself more fully to Jesus, John, and Paul.

The question remains, however, as to the extent to which one may consider the Old Testament a "Christian" document. From one point of view, it cannot be denied that the Old Testament was the product of ancient Judaism and has always been the sacred book of that religion. It is only by a strained exegesis that one may find a "Christology" in the Old Testament, or anything more than a foundation for later Christianity. But, from another point of view, the entire Bible is seen as the history of God's work of salvation, and from this perspective neither the Old Testament nor the New Testament is complete without the other. The coming of Christ is foreshadowed in the Old Testament, and in him the promises of the Old Testament are fulfilled.

It is this latter view which has perhaps been most characteristic of Christian faith, although an emphasis upon the Jewishness of the Old Testament is certainly not incompatible with Christian interpretation! What the Christian must be most careful about is the misleading tendency to read into Old Testament passages a specifically Christian content. To say that the Old Testament has relevance for Christian faith is one thing; to say that the original meaning was Christological is quite another.

We are not so much concerned in this book with a Christian understanding of the Old Testament as with the problem of discovering the Old Testament understanding of God. Once this has been achieved one may go on to a discussion of the relation of this understanding to Christian faith. The objection has been raised that one cannot discover what the Old Testament really says about God except by approaching the problem from a Christian perspective. That is to say that the New Testament is essential to the understanding of the Old Testament. This much may be granted, certainly for those whose commitment is to the Christian way.

Even for the Christian, however, such an approach is not entirely sufficient. As some commentators have observed, for most if not all of us, the normal path to a genuine understanding of the New Testament is by way of the Old. We can insist, therefore, that the Old Testament is essential to the understanding of the New Testament, a conviction that underlies the viewpoint of the present book. In the chapters that follow, however, it will be evident that our primary concern is to let the Old Testament understanding of God speak for itself.

I

God in Early Hebrew Thought

THE OLD TESTAMENT SOURCES

Part of the problem of understanding what the earliest Hebrews thought about God is determining what are the earliest sources in the Old Testament. We cannot simply assume that the accounts of the first events are our oldest records, for these accounts were in most cases not written until centuries after the events they record. Scarcely any of the Biblical writings are actually contemporary with the periods that they describe or record.

Yet there is much in the Old Testament that genuinely represents antiquity and that gives us a very real insight into the earliest Hebrew thought. There are ancient poems and prayers, snatches of songs, primitive stories and folklore, and there is even some evidence of very early religious thinking and practice, elements of which predate the age of the first known Hebrews by many generations. As examples of the latter we may note Hebrew parallels to ancient Mesopotamian myths of creation, giants, and the flood, and such reminiscences of primitive religion as reverence for springs, trees, and stones, and perhaps even human sacrifice.

The task of discovering the oldest fragments of religious material in the Old Testament and determining their approximate age was the primary concern of Old Testament literary analysis until recent decades. The most fruitful work in this field of study had been the separation of Old Testament writings, especially the Pentateuch, into independent literary documents or sources. The chief result of this research was the identification of at least four major strands of written material, the earliest of which can be dated to the tenth century B.C.[1] In each of these literary strands, however, there is certainly some material that originated many centuries before the written document that now contains it. Nevertheless, we must continually remind ourselves that almost everything in the Old Testament was *written* later than the tenth century B.C.

The investigation of the preliterary stages of Old Testament poetry, folk story, legend, and other material involves the study of the history of oral transmission—the handing down from generation to generation by word of mouth of usually unwritten traditions. That such a process of transmission was common among many ancient peoples is well attested not only in the Near East, but also in the Far East, Scandinavia, and elsewhere. In the case of the Old Testament, research into the oral traditions behind our written documents has proved invaluable not only in establishing the approximate age and time of origin of many sections of the literature, but also in understanding their original context and the situations that helped to produce them.

Thus we can approach the problem of setting the Old Testament writings into a general chronological line with reasonable confidence. We cannot be sure in all cases that a certain literary work preceded or followed another in a precise order, but we can place the material in its approximate time period. This makes it possible to speak of "early Hebrew thought," although one must recognize that the history of thought is much more difficult to delineate than is the history of literature. Nevertheless, the understanding of God in the thinking of the earliest Hebrews is available to us if we approach the subject with proper care and thorough study.

In speaking of early Hebrew thought, we must arbitrarily draw a line in order to specify particularly the end of the early period. The beginning of it is open, since we will want to find the most ancient ideas now contained in the Old Testament, but its terminal point must be fixed. Since with Moses there is clearly a new direction and emphasis in the development of Old Testament thought, his period (thirteenth century B.C.) is the most logical terminal point. "Early Hebrew thought," then, means everything that is considered to be pre-Mosaic in origin.

The difficulty with this demarcation of time is that almost every Old Testament tradition and writing was affected in its composition and transmission by the experiences of Moses' time, and this forces us to recognize that even our earliest sources were written, as it were, through a glass on which Moses and the exodus from Egypt are deeply etched. Since the exodus was the pivotal event in Israel's religious history, it inevitably conditioned everything that followed it, that is, everything after about the thirteenth century B.C. All of the Old Testament written tradition, which had its real beginning only in the tenth century, was thus produced under the shadow of this mighty act of God. Failure to take into account this significant factor would be to misunderstand seriously the nature of our Old Testament sources.

On the basis of what has been said above, and utilizing the researches of many students of the Old Testament, we can offer at least a general suggestion concerning the Old Testament writings that represent the earliest Hebrew thinking, keeping in mind that some of these traditions have been influenced by the events of the exodus period. Among the earliest Old Testament materials are several poems and poetic fragments, found for the most part in the Pentateuch. A few of these may reflect an age earlier than Moses, but most of them are clearly from his time or later. Only the primitive Song of Lamech (Gen. 4:23–24) is definitely pre-Mosaic.

Of somewhat more interest is the legal material preserved in the Pentateuch, some of which, even though attributed to Moses, is demonstrably from an earlier period. The Book of the Covenant in Ex. 20:22 to 23:19 contains much that is similar to the ancient laws in the Code of Hammurabi (eighteenth century B.C.). These laws may have been known to the earliest Hebrews in Mesopotamia or may have been transmitted to them in part by their Canaanite neighbors. In any case, the laws offer only limited insight into the understanding of the earliest Hebrew theology.

Traditions embedded in the book of Genesis provide the most

helpful sources for the understanding of God in early Hebrew thought. While these narratives, in their present written form, are no earlier than the tenth century B.C., and some are much later than that, in many cases they still genuinely reflect ancient ideas about God. It is impossible to date these ideas, but, as we shall see, in some instances they may go back to Near Eastern traditions as old as 2000 B.C. The relationship of some of these Old Testament stories to their ancient milieu will be considered in subsequent discussions.

THE MILIEU OF THE ANCIENT NEAR EAST

Hebrew thought and culture cannot be described and understood apart from its total Near Eastern context. This is especially important for understanding the earliest periods of the Old Testament, but it has relevance for later periods as well.

The place of Hebrew society in the ancient world and the cross-cultural influences that helped to determine its development have become increasingly clear through recent study. So much effort has gone into this kind of research, and so many parallels have been found between the thought and life of the Old Testament and that of contemporary Near Eastern cultures that it has become necessary to speak cautiously lest one be guilty of overstating the case. Nevertheless, there is much of value to be learned in this field, and we may note a few such points of contact in the following discussion.

Many legends, laws, and myths of the Old Testament share in a common cultural heritage with the ancient peoples of Canaan, Phoenicia, Syria, Anatolia, and Mesopotamia. The classical Sumerian culture of lower Mesopotamia (ca. 2800–2400 B.C.) provided a rich store of traditions which were the common property of many Near Eastern groups, including the Hebrews of the Old Testament. Stories of the creation of the world and man, of great ancestors and heroes of the past, of a terrible flood that devastated the earth, and of man's many achievements (buildings, cities, languages, etc.) are found among most of these groups, often in very similar forms. That the Old Testament stories are somehow different, because they are the product of a special people with a special relationship to God, does not alter the fact that the Old Testament narratives owe a great deal to this widely shared reservoir of ancient thought.

The early Hebrew concept of deity was undoubtedly influenced, if not largely determined, by this ancient cultural milieu. The oldest known Mesopotamian ideas about the gods are not entirely dissimilar from certain concepts of God found in Genesis. Polytheism was an ever-present reality in the ancient Near East, and its appearance in the pages of the Old Testament should be no surprise. The names of the gods of Mesopotamia have much in common with divine names in the Old Testament, and there is considerable evidence of the process of syncretism.[2]

Yet, the Hebrew view of God is different, perhaps even in pre-Mosaic thought, and certainly in the thought of the writers of Genesis. Although the Hebrews adopted older ideas and stories, they also *adapted* these traditions to their own view, and thus a new and unique religious tradition was formed. As examples, it is instructive to compare briefly the Hebrew and Babylonian stories of creation and of the great flood.

The Babylonian creation story (called *Enuma Elish*, "When above") presupposes the same general cosmology as that of Gen., ch. 1, including the primeval watery chaos. But the Babylonian story pictures these original waters in terms of personified powers, that is to say, divine beings. The primary act of creation of sky and earth is accomplished not by fiat, not by the spoken word of God, but by the violent slaughter of the chief sea monster at the hands of the powerful god Marduk. Despite its literary merits, the story is theologically "primitive" throughout.

By contrast, the adaptation of this story in Gen., ch. 1, displays much more developed concepts, and even though the present form of the story is a product of much later times, we can assume that the early Hebrews were already moving toward these higher concepts. The God of Genesis is all-powerful, although he is not alone, as the use of "us" and "our" in Gen. 1:26 (also ch. 3:22) indicates. The plural forms undoubtedly refer to divine beings who were thought to dwell with God, although they were not equal with God. In Genesis, God creates by the power of his spoken word. Everything that he makes he considers to be good, and his creative acts reach their climax in the making of man and in the setting aside of a day of rest, an obvious product of the later priestly emphasis on the Sabbath.

A more "primitive" account of creation is found in Gen., ch. 2, where the order of events is quite different from that of Gen., ch. 1. But the whole underlying concept of God is also different, and this concept will need to be elaborated further in another part of this chapter. The central concern of this fascinating story is man—where he came from, what he is, and why he does as he does. It has less specific contact with the Babylonian epic, but shares much of its theology and cosmology.

In the Biblical flood story we also find interesting parallels with Babylonian literature, as well as significant differences. The narratives in Gen., chs. 6 to 9, are from the "Yahwist" (J) tradition, first recorded in about the tenth century B.C. by Judean writers, but undoubtedly based upon epical sources, largely oral, from much earlier times. When we look at the Babylonian flood story, from about 2000 B.C., it becomes obvious that the Genesis story is simply another version of this mighty event.

The Babylonian story of the flood is part of the great Gilgamesh Epic, a literary masterpiece that has been called the "Odyssey" of the Babylonians. The hero of the epic, Gilgamesh, was a legendary Sumerian king who in time was deified in Sumerian mythology. In one episode of the epic, Gilgamesh sought out Ut-napishtim, the Babylonian Noah, who had, however, attained immortality and entered into the company of the gods. Ut-napishtim relates the lengthy story of the great deluge, telling of an ark ordered by his god, into which he gathered his family and a selection of animals; the coming of the flood, which lasted only seven days but was universal in its destructiveness; the ark's landing upon a mountain; the sending out of a dove; and the sacrifice of thanksgiving and propitiation offered upon returning to dry land.

These and other parallels indicate the closeness of the Hebrew and Babylonian versions of the flood, both of which are probably dependent upon an earlier Sumerian account.[3] But the two versions are significantly different at the point that most concerns us, namely, the understanding of the nature of deity.

In Genesis only God (Yahweh) directs the events of the flood and the affairs of Noah; no other gods are involved, as in Babylonia. Furthermore, there is a strong ethical theme running through the Genesis story, but such a theme is completely lacking in the Babylonian account. God sent the flood as punishment upon wicked mankind; only the righteous Noah and his family were saved. Before the flood, God even gave man an opportunity to turn back from his sinful ways, which he did not do. After the Deluge, God made a covenant with all his creatures never again to destroy the earth by a flood. In the sacrifice scene after the flood, God accepted the sweet fragrance of the offering made by Noah, whereas Ut-napishtim's sacrifice is depicted as necessary food for the hungry gods, who had not been fed by the sacrifices for some time, and who "gathered like flies over the sacrificer."

These and other differences between the two versions of the great Deluge show clearly how the Hebrews adapted early Mesopotamian material to their own purpose and point of view. The study of the stories of creation, the Tower of Babel, and lesser narratives in Genesis reinforces the point. Thus we can acquire an understanding of how the Biblical narratives came out of the milieu of the ancient Near East, but in most cases departed significantly from it.

ANTHROPOMORPHISM

We come now to a persistent problem in research on early Hebrew thought about God, the problem of anthropomorphism. This matter was referred to briefly in the preceding chapter in the discussion of the "language" of the Old Testament, and we shall need to consider it more carefully at this point.

Theology is concerned with communicating ideas *about* God; it does not claim to communicate God. It is necessary to keep this fundamental idea in mind if we are to understand Old Testament thought about God. There is the recognition, even in early Hebrew theology, that God is really ineffable; hence, the eventual prohibition of images that might attempt to capture his "likeness." God is not absolutely remote and transcendent, but he cannot be fully defined or described. All such attempts to delineate or categorize the being of God ultimately result in a being who is not God. We may say that in the Old Testament, God is everywhere apprehended, but he is nowhere comprehended.

Yet man must somehow talk about God and endeavor to express his experience of that which to him is Wholly Other, ineffable and incomprehensible. And to do so, in theological terms, inevitably results in anthropomorphism, that is, putting the infinite into finite concepts, expressing the nature of pure Being in the language of human existence, and using those words and terms which convey meaning in the thinking of the creature man (*anthrōpos*). It is part of the limitation of human thought that such means of communication must be employed as we attempt to bring the ultimate more concretely into the penultimate levels of our human existence. Since we must use the concepts and language of which we are capable, we do so in the full awareness of their limitations, thus preventing our thinking that when we talk about God we have somehow captured him within our system of thought.

All the references to God in the preceding sections are obviously and admittedly anthropomorphic. We have no other effective way of referring to God, even when objectively describing the problem of theological communication. Religious language is always anthropomorphic, and in this respect the Old Testament is no exception. This way of speaking about God is certainly not confined to the earliest times, as though the problem was exclusively one of primitive religious experience. But it is important to recognize the anthropomorphic dimension of Old Testament thought at the outset, so that we may be aware of its implications throughout our survey of the Old Testament understanding of God.

Anthropomorphism in the Old Testament is most apparent in the books of the Pentateuch, although it is certainly not absent from the prophetic literature, the historical works, and the other writings. Genesis is a good illustration of the common use of anthropomorphic language. In the Yahwist (J) account of creation in Gen., chs. 2 and 3, a tenth-century adaptation of much older myths, God is depicted as molding man from the dust of the ground, breathing life into his nostrils, building woman from man's rib, and walking and talking in the Garden of Eden "in the cool of the day."

As the Genesis narrative continues with events beyond the garden, one is struck by the frequent inclusion of "conversations" between God and various persons. It seems perfectly natural to the writer that God would speak to a man and that the man would reply, as though such a divine-human conversation were not at all unusual. So it is with Cain in Gen., ch. 4, with Noah in Gen., chs. 6 to 9, and with the patriarchs throughout the bulk of Genesis. No attempt is made to examine or to explain how such discourse occurs; early Hebrew thought takes for granted that God and man should communicate freely!

Many examples of anthropomorphic usage can be cited from the pages of the Old Testament, both from early and from later material. What the reader should have clearly in mind when he encounters such usage is that this is a legitimate expression of man's attempt to know God and to talk about him. There is little point in raising the question whether God "really said that," or in wondering if God is really like that. In the Old Testament records we have an authentic account of a people's faith response and of their understanding of the Being they knew as God. It should be sufficient for us to accept this understanding for what it is and to strive to increase our own insight by means of it.

GOD AND THE CREATION

Here we will want to consider more fully the understanding of God found in the earliest creation story in Genesis. In general, scholars agree that the account of creation in Gen. 1:1 to 2:4a is in its present form a Priestly (P) version that must be dated in the sixth century B.C. As such it presents the somewhat more sophisticated view of later generations and should not be considered representative of pre-Mosaic thought, except that it preserves elements of an earlier myth of creation known throughout Mesopotamia.

Of more immediate interest to us is the account of the creation found in Gen. 2:4b–24, which is much more closely akin to ancient mythic thought, although it owes its present form to the Yahwist writer of the tenth century B.C. Precisely at what point in time this story first became a part of Hebrew tradition we cannot now say. But it is surely old enough to serve as a good indicator of early Hebrew thinking about God as the Creator.

The story has often been called naïve and primitive in its theological understanding, and it does indeed depict God in rather simple anthropomorphic terms. It must not be thought, however, that the author (or authors) of the Yahwist epic of creation was lacking in wisdom or profoundness of insight. On the contrary, there is here a richness of feeling for the human condition and for the God-man relationship that makes this story a classic of religious literature. The reasons for this judgment will be apparent as we consider some of its outstanding features.

God is understood in Gen., ch. 2, to be the absolute Lord of existence. He is Lord because he is Creator. As the story begins, God has made the earth and the heavens, but as yet no *living* thing—we might say, no organic matter—has been created. His first act of creation is to form man (*'adam*) of the dust from the ground and to breathe into him the breath of life. Thus man became the first living being. The explicit relationship here between the breath of God and the life of man is of great significance, and will be elaborated more fully in the section on "The Spirit of God." What should be noted at this point is the primacy of man in the sequence of creation; he was made first, before all other living things. Only after man had been formed did God turn to the creating of plants and animals.

Next, God planted a garden "in Eden," or "of Eden," which is located by the author "in the east," presumably in Mesopotamia. The garden was planted for man to enjoy, with certain specific restrictions, but man also was put in the garden to till it and to keep it. Concern for man's physical well-being is clearly expressed in this part of the story. Concern for man's psychic well-being is also expressed in God's recognition that it is not good for man to be alone, the only one of his kind. Thus God created (literally, "formed") all of the living creatures—the beasts of the field and the birds of the air. Since none of these was found to be a suitable helper for the man, the Lord God had to make another manlike creature, a woman, who was bone of his bones and flesh of his flesh.

The continuation of this narrative of creation is the temptation story in Gen., ch. 3. Here anthropomorphism is rife, and the mythology contains elements of fable and perhaps reflections of animal worship. The serpent motif, for example, is frequently found in ancient Near Eastern religious literature and practice.

There are also several etiologies in this remarkable chapter of Genesis, such as those which give a primitive explanation of the origin of human disobedience, the knowledge of sex, the incompatibility of snakes and people, the pain of woman in childbirth, and man's days of toil. The account was certainly not written merely to express a particular view of such matters, but etiologies do form an important part of the Yahwist's material here and elsewhere in Genesis.

The explanatory elements, however, are subordinate to the theological purpose of the author. He is proclaiming in his own special way a people's belief about the meaning of existence, and, more specifically, about the relationship between God the Creator and man the creature. This is a twofold relationship. On the one hand, God is very close to his creatures. He walks in the garden in the cool of the day and seeks out the man and the woman. He converses with them and treats them like the wayward and disobedient children they are. They know that he is near to them. On the other hand, they are not to be permitted to share fully in the knowledge of good and evil that originally belonged only to God. Their days on earth are to be limited—the tree of life also being forbidden to them—so that they do not have the immortality of the gods. And, since they were formed out of the dust, their abode is earth, not heaven.

Although the idea of God the Creator is not confined to the Genesis stories, it is here that we find the greatest expression of that idea in the Old Testament. So much of what man has for centuries believed about the origin of life and the physical universe is based upon that expression. Many misconceptions, too, have resulted from inadequate interpretation of the creation story. Nevertheless, the meaningful religious truths that are at the heart of the Genesis narrative, truths about the nature of existence and the relationship between God and man, may still be discerned and may still inform our understanding of God.

GOD AND NATURE

We have noted that the earliest view of God and his creation attempts to maintain a balance between God's immanence and his transcendence with reference to the created order. Is there beyond this a consistent way of looking at the relationship between God and nature in the earliest portions of the Old Testament?

The ancient Hebrew world view was essentially mythological. It came out of an age and a culture that were prelogical and pre-scientific, as we understand logic and science today, and whose ideas were most often expressed in mythological language. The term "mythological" is used here to refer to the symbolic and approximate expression of those truths which the human mind does not perceive clearly but can only glimpse vaguely, and therefore cannot adequately or accurately express.[4] Our earliest sources are consistently mythological in the sense of this definition, and we have already observed (above, pp. 21 f.) that myth is an important genre in Old Testament literature.

In Genesis the earth is depicted as a flat disk. A firmament overhead, like an inverted bowl, holds out the waters above, and beneath the earth there are also oceans of water (the great deeps). The sources of the great Deluge, according to Genesis, are "the fountains of the deep" and "the windows of the heavens" (Gen. 7:11; 8:2). The early Hebrew concept of the universe is both geocentric and anthropocentric. There is no idea of limitless space, and man is made the measure of all things in nature.

Where is God in this cosmology? For the most part he resides in the heavens or the sky, presumably around the firmament. He comes *down* to earth when he appears to man, and to this extent is personal and immanent. But he is not in nature; he is its creator and is to be distinguished from it. The Biblical view is never pantheistic or monistic. It is always theistic.

There is a very important distinction between the Biblical idea of God as creator of the natural world and the general ancient Near Eastern idea of the gods as part of nature. In the Old Testament, God is never represented as a natural force. He is not the sun, moon, or stars, the earthquake, wind, or flood. These objects and forces of nature may represent him, his power and his will, but he is not in them. He orders and controls them as their creator and Lord.

Early Hebrew man may well have worshiped at trees, springs, and stones, but the Old Testament now preserves only reflections of such worship. A reconstruction of primitive religion from Old Testament sources is theoretically possible, but our interest here is in the dominant point of view preserved in the Biblical writings, admittedly the result of postprimitive reflection and maturity. Thus, in early Hebrew thought, we find God already understood as separate from nature, its creator and ruler.

THE SPIRIT OF GOD

No concept of God in the Old Testament is more rooted in primitive thought than the idea of the spirit of God. Its association with early man's way of thinking about the nonmaterial world is evident in several passages from the oldest Old Testament sources. This does not mean that the idea was given up in later times, however, for the original concept proved to be so instructive that it was retained in a variety of forms in later thought. Here we are concerned with the expression of this idea in its earliest forms.

At the outset it is necessary to note that early Hebrew thought had not arrived at a general understanding of God as spirit. That is to say, there is no metaphysical assertion that God is pure spirit, that the nature or substance of his being is purely nonmaterial. Not even in later Old Testament writings or in the New Testament do we find such speculation about the nature of God, although the saying that "God is spirit," attributed to Jesus in John 4:24, may be based upon some such assumption. In general, the Biblical writers prefer to speak of "the spirit of God," "God's spirit," or "the Holy Spirit."

In the Old Testament the word most frequently translated "spirit" is *ruach*, a Hebrew word having a variety of meanings. It can mean "breath," "wind," "air," "spirit," "disposition." It can refer to the breath or spirit of any animate being or to the spirit of God.[5] Early man's reflection upon the source of his life as an animate being led him to make an association between the breath or air that vitalized him within and the spirit that he sensed in the world about him. This is precisely the association we find in the earliest stages of Old Testament thought.

Again, our best source for an early expression of Hebrew religious thought is Genesis. In Gen. 1:2 it is the spirit or wind of God that moves over (literally, "broods over") the face of the waters, and even though the material here was shaped by the later Priestly editors, it still represents a primitive stage of the religious understanding of God and his involvement in the work of creation. The concept of a divine wind brooding over the primordial watery chaos suggests an extension of the being of God himself, and as such is somewhat different from the idea of God creating simply by the power of his spoken word.

Of even more interest is the passage in the Yahwist's account of creation, wherein the origin of human life is attributed to the breath or spirit of God: "Then the LORD God formed man of dust from the ground, and breathed into his nostrils the breath of life; and man became a living being" (Gen. 2:7).

Here "breath" is not merely a detached representation of God, but is that part of his vital being which gives vitality or life to man. The picture here given is intensely personal and anthropomorphic. God not only formed man from the ground, as a potter shapes his clay, but he also animated man by his own life-giving spirit. As a result, man became a living being. The Hebrew words used here may mean "soul," "living being," "life," "self," "person," but they usually refer to man in his totality as a living being. Thus the spirit or vital principle of God's being constitutes man a whole psychophysical self.

Elsewhere in early Hebrew thought the spirit of God is chiefly a representation of the manner of God's appearing to or dealing with men. God appears in various "spiritual" forms, as messengers, angels, or men. Of course, the direct manifestation of God, especially in speaking, is the primary mode of his self-communication with his people. But in the patriarchal traditions (Gen., chs. 12 to 50) there are occasional appearances of God as some kind of spiritual agent. The "angel of the Lord" came to Hagar in the wilderness (Gen. 16:7 ff.). God appeared to Abraham and Sarah as "three men" (Gen., ch. 18) and to Lot as "two angels" or "messengers" (Gen., ch. 19). An "angel of the Lord" called to Abraham from heaven to prevent his sacrifice of Isaac (Gen. 22:11 ff.). In an intriguing passage in Gen. 32:22-32, Jacob wrestled during the night with "a man," a divine being presumably sent by God. This legend contains the story of Jacob's name being changed to Israel, which the writer understands to mean "he who strives with God." Jacob is reported to have said at the conclusion of this incident, "I have seen God face to face."

Although in none of these examples do we find the phrase "spirit of God," the underlying assumption of all such references is that the intangible nature of God may be represented by beings who appear quite real to men. God is not abstract and impersonal. Man finds him in whatever individual and personal experience he believes to be touched by divinity. The spirit of God is everywhere present and impresses itself upon certain divine moments. How this understanding was to develop and become a dominant way of seeing God's activity in human history will be considered in later chapters.

THE GOD OF THE FATHERS

In the pre-Mosaic period the real history of the people of God begins with Abraham. The legends of Gen., chs. 12 to 50, contain the kernel of the patriarchal history, the stories of Abraham, Isaac, Jacob, and Joseph. These "fathers" of the nation knew God and enjoyed a special covenant relationship with him, according to the tradition of the Pentateuch.

It is the understanding of these traditions that Yahweh, as God was later known by Moses, was also the God of Abraham, Isaac, and Jacob. According to Ex. 6:2–4 (P; cf. E in Ex. 3:6): "And God said to Moses, 'I am the LORD. I appeared to Abraham, to Isaac, and to Jacob, as God Almighty, but by my name the LORD I did not make myself known to them. I also established my covenant with them, to give them the land of Canaan, the land in which they dwelt as sojourners.'" How do the narratives about the patriarchs in Genesis accord with this understanding? Since the patriarchal narratives have obviously been worked over in the light of the Sinai traditions, including the exodus from Egypt and the covenant at Mt. Sinai, they generally point toward these later events as part of a unified view of God in history. Another tradition, incorporated in the Yahwist epic, holds that it was Yahweh who created all things, selected Abraham and his descendants, and led his people out of Egypt in the time of Moses. This is, in brief, the Israelite credo concerning Yahweh.

A more searching analysis of the Genesis traditions reveals a somewhat different historical situation. Beneath the smoothly elaborated surface of the Yahwist-Elohist story we discover traces of what may once have been tribal deities. Since later literary reworking has somewhat obscured the earlier traditions, conclusions about the nature of patriarchal religion are necessarily tentative, but scholars have succeeded in drawing a rather convincing picture.

Exodus 6:2 states that Yahweh was known to the fathers of Israel as El Shaddai, meaning "God Almighty" or "God of the Mountains." It is clear that this name, as well as others, was commonly used to designate the God of the fathers (see Gen. 17:1; 28:3; 35:11; 48:3; 49:25). He is also identified by such titles as El Elyon ("God Most High"), El Olam ("God Everlasting"), El Roi ("God of Seeing"), and El Bethel ("God of the House of God").

Thus, in view of this situation, it is necessary to speak of the *gods* of the fathers, for there is further evidence that each of the patriarchs was associated with the deity in a very special individual relationship. In each case the deity has also a special name indicating his relationship with the patriarch: the "Shield of Abraham" (Gen. 15:1), the "Kinsman of Isaac" (Gen. 31:42, 53), and the "Mighty One of Jacob" (Gen. 49:24). Instead of the God of Abraham, Isaac, and Jacob, we have the God of Abraham, the God of Isaac, and the God of Jacob![6]

This view of the gods of the fathers of Israel does justice to the Biblical traditions, but at the same time poses the problem of polytheism. But perhaps the problem is largely in our own preconception of the nature of Biblical thought about the Deity, based in part upon the Yahwist's overview of God in history. The fact remains that according to Genesis the patriarchs acknowledged several deities, as the names cited above indicate, and perhaps even others not mentioned in Genesis. The argument that these were but different names for the one God of Israel fails to take adequate account of the realities of primitive religion and of the evidence from Biblical tradition.

In time a process of syncretism did begin to identify the various patriarchal deities with Yahweh, the God of Israel who first made himself known to Moses. The old names and titles were gradually forgotten or dropped, and the classic retelling of Israel's story by the Yahwist and later by the Elohist completed the process of elevating Yahweh to the position of Israel's God from the beginning. Thus in Gen., ch. 2 (J), it was Yahweh who created the earth, the heavens, and all living things.

What is important about the patriarchal concept of God is that it was susceptible of being adapted to the later insistence on the sole legitimacy of Yahweh. The Biblical writers did not sense any conflict between the God of Moses and the God of the fathers, nor did they find it difficult to understand that Yahweh was the God, by whatever name, who was actively present throughout the history of Israel, even from the beginning at creation. This is basic to the faith of Israel, and it is impossible to understand the Old Testament view of God apart from this fundamental fact.

II

The God of Moses

TRADITIONS OF THE REVELATION OF YAHWEH TO MOSES

We begin this chapter with a brief description of the Old Testament literary traditions, especially in Exodus, that provide a basis for our knowledge of Hebrew religion in the time of Moses (early thirteenth century B.C.). It is necessary to do this because of our interest in the chronological development of the idea of God in the Old Testament, recognizing all the while that there are limitations to such a procedure.

The book of Exodus is of central importance for the understanding of God in the Mosaic period. It preserves fragments of very ancient songs and stories that seem to have sprung directly from the actual events which they depict. Such major Israelite themes as the exodus from Egypt, the covenant at Mt. Sinai, and the wilderness wandering, are also captured in traditions that now provide a major part of the substance of Exodus.

In Exodus we are dealing with a very complex document, just as in the case of Genesis. A variety of oral traditions have been identified in the book, stemming from several different groups and places. The stories about the young Moses, for example, seem to have originated independently of the accounts of later events; the collections of laws are not originally from one unified source; there are different versions of the same event and different names for the same people, and so on. But these diverse materials, all related to the three major themes just mentioned, were eventually brought together into one major written work, the book of Exodus.

Still, there are at least two significant versions of the common traditions in Exodus that must be recognized, the Yahwist (J) and the Elohist (E).[1] In addition to these two, the later Priestly (P) source is also represented in the book, notably in the historical and legal material, and must be carefully distinguished from its earlier counterparts. In all probability, the J and E versions of the events recorded in Exodus both came from a common oral tradition, but were adapted in written form to the religious needs and convictions of the specific situations in which the Yahwist and Elohist writers found themselves. For J, this situation was most likely the time of rising "nationalism" in the reigns of David and Solomon (tenth century B.C.), a time when the identity of Israel as the nation of God led many to become more interested in their historical origins and past. In the case of E, a northern prophetic writer of the eighth century compiled and edited this material as an expression of the particular religious views of the northern tribes of Israel.

Both J and E are controlled by the central affirmation of faith in Yahweh as the God of Israel. They do not agree, however, on one of the essential points in the story of Israel's relationship to Yahweh. Simply stated, the Elohist tradition assumes that God was not known to the Israelites by any one personal name until he revealed himself to Moses as "Yahweh" (Ex. 3:13-15).[2] The Yahwist account disagrees completely with this Moses-Yahweh tradition by using the divine name Yahweh for God throughout the J history, notably in Genesis and Exodus. Many other differences in detail and point of view make it clear that both versions of Israel's history in Exodus are crucial to an understanding of the God of Moses.

Although much attention has been focused upon Moses in the Exodus accounts, it is Yahweh, not Moses, who is the "hero" or central figure in the story. Moses plays his role, to be sure, and his contribution to Israel's history and religion should not be minimized. In the Exodus traditions, however, his part has undoubtedly been maximized. But Moses acts only in *response* to Yahweh, as in his acceptance of the divine call to lead his people (Ex., chs. 3; 4). Yahweh acts; he commands Moses and the Israelites; he instructs and uplifts and delivers them from oppression and danger. Throughout the history of the Mosaic era attention focuses upon Yahweh rather than upon Moses.

We must remember, too, that in Exodus we are not reading history so much as an interpretation of events seen and remembered through faith. The story of the God of Moses is a type of "history" that includes original events intermingled with later interpretations, some of which are as late as the sixth century B.C., or about six centuries after Moses! This faith-interpreted history cannot, of course, be "verified" by the usual historical means. Archaeology, for example, offers only the most general kind of confirmation for this period. Instead, the verification for such a history is found in the ongoing faith of Israel itself, and in the continuing response to that faith in the entire Judeo-Christian tradition.

THE ORIGINS OF YAHWISM

Having acknowledged that the accounts of the God of Moses in Exodus are traditional in nature, we must nevertheless attempt to learn something of the actual origins of Yahweh religion. Just because our sources are traditional, and lacking in factual detail, whatever we can learn about the roots of Yahwism will be profitable for our understanding of this period. It is clear that the religion of Moses was in large measure a product of its time and place, and we must always keep that specific context in mind.

The Elohist's account of the beginnings of Yahwism provides us with a tradition that is probably closest to actual fact. As we have noted above, this story tells of God's confronting Moses on Horeb (Sinai), the "mountain of God" in Midian. Here Moses was told that the name of God was YHWH, that is, "Yahweh" (Ex. 3:13–15). The name appears to mean "He Causes to Be" or "I Cause to Be." We cannot say what the name may have meant to others who possibly knew it before Moses, but in this case its meaning for Hebrew faith is clear enough. God is the One who acts and causes to happen whatever happens in the life and history of his people.

Scholars have frequently speculated upon the possible origins of the Yahweh cult, for there is some evidence to indicate that it was not original with Moses and the Hebrew people. One of the most striking facts in the Exodus narrative of early Yahwism is that Jethro, the priest of Midian and Moses' father-in-law (Ex. 18:10), was apparently already an officiant in the Yahweh cult before Moses came along. It was in Midian on the mountain of God that Moses first came to know Yahweh (according to E). Jethro could then have instructed Moses in the ways of Yahweh religion, or perhaps had so instructed him even before the theophany of the burning bush on Mt. Horeb.

Following the exodus from Egypt, Moses led his people to the vicinity of Kadesh, in the Negeb region south of Canaan proper. There they were met by Jethro, to whom Moses "did obeisance," and there Jethro presided at a ceremony of burnt offering and sacrifices to God, with Aaron and the elders of Israel participating in the sacred meal (Ex. 18:12). There also Jethro suggested a most important innovation in the judicial organization of the people. Moses had been trying to settle all the disputes and answer all the questions brought to him by the people, and this had become an almost intolerable burden. Jethro counseled Moses to choose able men to serve as rulers and judges over divisions of the people by thousands, hundreds, fifties, and tens, with Moses handling only the weightiest problems. This system proved to be effective, and the tradition clearly attributes it to Jethro, rather than to Moses.

Additional support for this Midianite[3] theory of the origins of Yahwism comes from Num. 10:29 ff., where Hobab (Jethro) was entreated by Moses to accompany the Israelites on their journey as a guide and source of blessing for them. The tradition of the seventy elders who were selected to assist Moses and to bear some of his burdens is also associated with this time (Num. 11:16–17, 24–25).

It is entirely possible, then, that significant ideas and practices in Moses' religion were taken over from the Midianites. Sacrifice, the sacred lot, the Ark of the Covenant, a rudimentary judicial system, and perhaps some laws were part of the heritage received by Israel from the land of Midian. Of greatest significance is the fact that Israel seems first to have been introduced to the God Yahweh, who was to become her national protector and benefactor, through Moses' experience with Midian.

The God of Moses was undoubtedly viewed in this period against the background of earlier Hebrew beliefs about the nature and person of God. The E tradition specifically makes this point in Ex. 3:6: "And he said, 'I am the God of your father, the God of Abraham, the God of Isaac, and the God of Jacob.'" So also the Priestly writer in Ex. 6:3 identifies Yahweh with the God of the patriarchs who was known as "God Almighty" (see above, pp. 41 f.). Both E and P are much later than the Mosaic period, to be sure, but the association of Yahweh with the earlier deity by Moses and his people makes sense, and there is little reason to doubt its authenticity. The name "Yahweh" simply represents a new phase of God's self-revelation, in Israelite thought at least, and the continuity of the new religion with the earlier one is assumed throughout this part of the Old Testament.

It is much more difficult to speculate about the possible influence of Egyptian religion upon the understanding of God in the time of Moses. In almost every respect the religion of ancient Egypt was so different from anything we find in the Old Testament that very little direct comparison can be made. Although the "monotheistic" religion of Akhnaton (Amenhotep IV, ca. 1375–ca. 1366 B.C.) certainly left some impression upon the Egyptian mind, it is doubtful that a causal relationship can be established between the thought of Akhnaton and the beliefs of Moses, although a few scholars have attempted to relate the two. Much to be preferred is the view that Yahwism sprang from the soil of Midian, developed its own special concepts and cultus in response to the needs of certain groups of Israelites, and was later identified with the indigenous religion of the "fathers" of the pre-Mosaic period. We have already seen how the authors of the Mosaic traditions dealt with this problem in part through the assertion that God was known as El Shaddai before revealing his name Yahweh to Moses.

THE CHARACTER OF YAHWEH

The nature of the God whom Moses presumably introduced to Israel is not easy to describe. In one sense, this entire book is an attempt to describe God as the people of the Old Testament knew him, and in a brief section on the "character" of Yahweh we can only suggest some of the more important ways of thinking about God in the time of Moses. The reader should understand, therefore, that these suggestions will be necessarily general and incomplete.

That Yahweh was preeminently seen as creator of the universe has been discussed in the preceding chapter. In the traditions of the Mosaic period this aspect of Yahweh's character was not emphasized, a fact that seems to indicate the post-Mosaic origin of the identification of Yahweh with the deity of the ancient creation myths. Even the later great "sermons" of Moses in Deuteronomy failed to speak of God as Creator. What was important to the Mosaic faith was that which follows from God's creatorhood, namely, his Lordship over all things. Here God is the Supreme Ruler of men, nations, and history, especially the history of Israel. As Ruler he commands, and they are to obey. In the arena of history Yahweh manipulates whatever he wills, although not in an absolute or deterministic manner, in order to bring about his desire for Israel. At the same time, Israel is free and may choose to disobey, as indeed she did repeatedly throughout her history.

The Lordship of Yahweh was predicated also upon his power and holiness. In Exodus and elsewhere Yahweh is associated with, and undoubtedly was originally identified with, the forces of nature (see Ex. 19:16 ff.). He is represented by the thunderstorm, with its wind, fire (lightning), rain and hail, and perhaps even by the earthquake. He is the God of the mountain, with its awesome latent (volcanic?) powers, and he could send floods, plagues, and other natural disasters. He is holy (Hebrew, *qadosh,* "holy," "sacred," "separate"), in the sense of the "numinous" or awesome aspect of deity, and as such is to be feared, with the meaning both of terror and of reverence (see below, Ch. VIII).

Such a deity, though Creator and Lord, could never have been understood as completely transcendent or wholly removed from the world of human experience, even though, as we have seen, his abode was thought to be in the heavens. God came *down* from his abode and made himself known in personal relations with man, not in some abstract idea of Person or Power or Being. To the Israelites he was known more for what he did than for what he was. Thus we find that verbs, rather than abstract nouns, are most often used in the Old Testament in reference to God. He loves, forgives, judges, saves, redeems, and so on. Furthermore, in anthropopathic language, he is a jealous God, as the Second Commandment warns us in connection with the prohibition of image-making (Ex. 20:5; Deut. 5:9). The God of the covenant relationship with Israel simply could not tolerate any action that would threaten the singularity of that covenant. This idea of God's concern for his people's loyalty is succinctly stated in Ex. 34:14: "For you shall worship no other god, for the LORD, whose name is Jealous, is a jealous God."

One other aspect of God's character that the Ten Commandments reveal is that of his justice and righteousness. Although the commandments are addressed by God to man, they tell us something of the nature of God also. Since Yahweh acted justly and righteously in his dealings with man, man is required to live by these virtues also. Everywhere in the Mosaic traditions Yahweh is found to be faithful, just, and righteous. In other words, he is an ethical Deity whose standards of behavior are the highest that Israel could conceive within the framework of her time and place. It goes without saying that these standards changed somewhat with the centuries,[4] but never was Yahweh understood to exemplify less than the highest in moral conduct, in contrast to the behavior of the gods of many other nations. The concept of ethical monotheism will be discussed in a later chapter on the prophetic views of God.

No Other Gods: Moses and Monotheism

The concept of monotheism—belief in the existence of only one God—has long been a problem to historians of religion, and especially so to those who have investigated this idea in the Old Testament. Perhaps the basic question is whether this idea is at all useful in describing any religion before the age of classical Greek thought from which the theoretical concept of monotheism, or at least the term, was derived. It is obviously anachronous to use a term devised in one period of history to describe a speculative concept which may have preceded that period by several centuries only in a pragmatic sense. There is no hint of theoretical monotheism in either the pre-Mosaic or Mosaic periods.

If it is assumed that some form of the Ten Commandments[5] was a product of Moses' time, then the first of these sayings would seem to be relevant to our problem: "You shall have no other gods before me."[6] Yet, just what is it that this First Commandment requires? It clearly requires only that primacy among the gods be given to Yahweh alone, so far as his people are concerned. The commandment assumes the existence of "other gods" who may be sovereign over other peoples (cf. Ex. 18:11; Num. 33:4), and it does not extend the primacy of Yahweh in a universal sense to all these other peoples. As we shall see in a later section, the commandments and laws of God in the Old Testament are meaningful primarily within the covenant relationship between God and Israel. But the existence of other gods was recognized in Moses' era, not in a polytheistic sense, but simply as a part of the general world view of that time and place. There was no explicit monotheism in the Mosaic period.

An explicitly monotheistic commandment would presumably read: "You shall *believe in* no other gods besides me." That is to say, belief in the existence of other gods than Yahweh is not acceptable. But nowhere in the literature or thought of this period do we find such an assertion. What we have, rather, is a type of religious belief and practice that has been called "henotheism,"[7] in which the sole legitimacy of one deity is central, but which does not theoretically deny the existence of all other deities. This concept is aptly descriptive of the religious situation of Israel in the time of Moses.[8]

Since in practice, if not in theory, Yahweh alone was God for Israel, we may speak of Mosaic faith as implicit monotheism. Such a term indicates that, on the practical level, Israel lived, or attempted to live, as though no other gods existed. Implicit monotheism was to be characteristic of Israel's religion from Moses' time to the time of Second Isaiah (sixth century B.C.).[9] The reinforcement of this practical, rather than conceptual, belief may be seen in the whole complex of covenants, commandments, and rituals that seem to have sprung from the Mosaic era. And it is further strengthened by the later institutions of monarchy, prophetism, and Temple cultus and priesthood that were the product in large measure of Israel's citied life in Canaan, which began soon after the death of Moses. To what extent Moses as an individual was responsible for the religion of Yahwism, either in its earlier or later manifestations, it is now impossible to determine. Perhaps it is best simply to say with others: If Moses had not existed, we would have to invent someone like him in order to account for the ideas and events of his time!

YAHWEH AND THE EXODUS FROM EGYPT

No single event in Israel's religious history was of more crucial significance than the exodus from Egypt. It is the central point of reference in the entire literature of the Old Testament, especially so in the historical and prophetic books, and to a lesser extent in the Writings. It is the event that most vividly revealed Yahweh as Israel's God acting in history, and it is this point of Israel's understanding of her God in the light of the exodus that is of most interest to us here. Moreover, in spite of the fact that the exodus traditions as we now have them are the product of later centuries, we can be confident that they still preserve the essence of Israel's faith in the time of Moses.

As we have said before, Israel's faith was almost exclusively a response to events, to what God did for and to them as a people. Israel came to know God because he acted in historical time as

Lord of history, and the exodus was the most meaningful act of God in Israel's long and troubled history. The exodus stands first for several reasons. For one, it strikingly demonstrated that Yahweh could and would intervene in human affairs to carry out his purposes. Again, it effectively revealed Yahweh's power and will to save his people and bless them, just as he had promised. Furthermore, out of the exodus came Israel herself, born in pain and travail and hope, as a new nation and a new religion. More than anything else, the exodus was a beginning, a new creation, for the heirs of Abraham.

The belief that Yahweh, a little-known desert God, could accomplish such things in the face of powerful Egypt was a daring one for ancient Israel, but without such a faith in the mighty acts of God there could have been no Israel. The story of the exodus probably contains more miracles than does any other chapter in the entire Old Testament history, as this was Israel's way of relating how God worked out his will for his people. This means simply that through the eyes of faith the ordinary and sometimes extraordinary events that took place in Egypt were seen as the work of God, as evidence of the manner in which he interceded on behalf of his people. Such events were then expressed in the religious language appropriate to that faith and to the world view of that time.[10]

In some of these events we seem to have the anomalous situation of Yahweh's working against his own purpose, as when he is said to have hardened Pharaoh's heart against Moses' request to let his people go (Ex. 4:21; 7:1-5; etc.). In reality, this view of things is additional evidence of Israel's belief that God both knew and controlled whatever was to happen in Israel's sacred history. Indeed, such a view is *Heilsgeschichte*, "sacred history" or "history of salvation." Thus Israel's special idea of God as One who acts in history[11] is emphasized again and again in the exodus story.

A theme dominant throughout the account of the exodus is that of Yahweh's compassion for his people's suffering. "I have seen the affliction of my people," God said to Moses. "I know their sufferings, and I have come down to deliver them out of the hand of the Egyptians." (Ex. 3:7-8.) God acted to deliver Israel out of her oppression, and in so doing his living, saving, blessing nature was forever inscribed deep in the faith of the Old Testament. That this loving and compassionate God of the Old Testament should have been so obscured by the image of an angry God of wrath and judgment is an unfortunate aspect of much popular Christian thought today. The quite proper prophetic picture of God's judgment upon Israel and the nations has too often been exaggerated in the contrast between the Old Testament "God of wrath" and the New Testament "God of love." Such a radical polarity of God's nature is a profound misunderstanding of the Bible. The careful student of Scripture will see a more correct view of the Biblical God as One in whom mercy and justice are equally weighty.

THE THEOPHANY AT MT. SINAI

Of the many occasions on which God manifested himself to Moses and the Israelites, none had more lasting import for Israel's subsequent religious history than the revelation at Sinai. There God made known not only his nature as a covenant-seeking God, but also his desire that Israel have an ordered structure in her religious life and worship.

The traditions in Ex. 19:1–25 and 20:18–21 concerning events at Sinai, the commandments in Ex. 20:1–17, and the "Covenant Code" in Ex. 20:22 to 23:19 have all been subjected to intensive literary criticism. Scholars have shown that laws in the Covenant Code are largely based on the ancient Code of Hammurabi (ca. 1728–1686 B.C.) and in their present form are the product of a settled agricultural community rather than of a nomadic desert group. We have already noted that the Decalogue, both in Exodus and in Deuteronomy, has been elaborated beyond its original, briefer form. The problem of what the giving of the law tells us about Moses' God, however, will be taken up in the next section.

The question here is: What did Israel come to understand about her God through the experience at Sinai? There is no reason to doubt that Moses and his people experienced some kind of happening there that made an indelible impression upon their corporate religious consciousness. This was not the first instance of Yahweh's speaking to the people through Moses, of course, but here at the sacred mountain, the very fount of Yahwism, they believed that Yahweh's self-revelation had reached new heights. At the very foundation of Israel's faith lay this belief that Yahweh would reveal himself, his nature and will, to his people. It is the *sine qua non* of early Yahwism. Moses is the first, and in a sense the most important, of God's mediators or prophets (i.e., spokesmen), whose task is that of communicating the divine word to the people. And it is to the *people* that God speaks, not simply to the spokesman. Thus, apart from the content of the revelation at Sinai, which we can no longer discover in detail, the most important element in the theophany is the reinforcement of the people's belief in the concept of Yahweh as a self-revealing God.

It may be said also, on the basis of this and similar experiences in Israel's history, that theophanic communication becomes normative to the faith of Israel. So far as the history of Yahwism is concerned, the exodus experience is fundamental and precedent-setting. Even though God had appeared in various guises and under various names to Moses' ancestors, something quite new and unique took place there in the wilderness. From that time there would be a new relationship between God and his people, a relationship that was to have structure and regularity and that was to issue in one of the world's great religions.

THE GOD OF COVENANT AND LAW

Thus far in our survey of the understanding of God in Moses' time the unasked and unanswered question has been: Why did God choose the Israelites in particular as his special people? We have seen that, even though Yahweh was believed to be identical with the God of the fathers, a radically new era in Hebrew religion began with the call of Moses and the exodus from Egypt. What did the Old Testament writers believe lay behind this dramatic new development?

In the Exodus account of the experience at Sinai the central event is the making of a covenant between Yahweh and Israel.

But the idea of a unilateral or suzerainty covenant between God and a particular people, unlike that of a bilateral or parity covenant between two men or two nations, presupposes God's initiative in making the agreement, that is to say, God's *election* of the people with whom he would covenant. God chose Israel; Israel did not choose God. The entire story of the Hexateuch[12] depends upon this fundamental belief, which became also a basic tenet of the Israelite credo. This tenet is assumed without explicit statement in Exodus, where the identification of Yahweh's acts in Moses' time with the acts of God in earlier times is a dominant theme. But in Deuteronomy, even though the original traditions have been interpreted in the light of later history, Moses reportedly made this statement to Israel: "For you are a people holy to the LORD your God; the LORD your God has chosen you to be a people for his own possession, out of all the peoples that are on the face of the earth. It was not because you were more in number than any other people that the LORD set his love upon you and chose you, for you were the fewest of all peoples; but it is because the LORD loves you, and is keeping the oath which he swore to your fathers, that the LORD has brought you out with a mighty hand, and redeemed you from the house of bondage, from the hand of Pharaoh king of Egypt" (Deut. 7:6–8). Thus God's love and his faithfulness to the Abrahamic promise are the reasons behind his election of Israel.

Earlier promises and covenants actually go back to Noah (Gen. 9:8–17) and to Abraham (Gen. 15:17–21, J; 17:1–14, P), the former being a universal contract between God and all mankind, whereas the latter is between God and Abraham's descendants. In later discussions, and in the last chapter of this book, we shall see that the covenant idea is vital to the meaning of the entire Bible.

Two versions of the Mosaic covenant are found in Exodus: one when the people first arrived at the sacred mountain in Sinai (chs. 19: 1–25; 20:18–21); the other just before Moses went up on the mountain for forty days and forty nights (ch. 24:1–18). The latter may be simply a ceremony ratifying the former, but in both cases Yahweh sought to bind Israel to him alone as their God, and the people solemnly agreed to be obedient to the Lord who had chosen them and promised to protect and bless them. In the latter account Moses also sealed the covenant with appropriate rituals of offerings and sacrifices.

From the time of covenant-making, there came traditionally the Book of the Covenant, which was apparently the major collection of covenant laws (Ex. 20:22 to 23:19). In the preceding section we noted that many of these laws are from times earlier or later than Moses, but the point here is not what source analysis tells us about the literature; it is what the concept of covenant law tells us about God. Simply stated, the laws associated with the covenant tell us what God requires of his people. The covenant relationship requires faithfulness[13] on the part of both God and the people, and the people's faithfulness is concretized in the commandments they have agreed to obey. Israel was always to look upon the law as a gracious gift from God, not as a repugnant and onerous obligation. It was God's means of providing a framework within which religious life could be properly carried on, in which the sacredness of life could be preserved, and in which a vital and lasting relationship with God could be established. Thus God's covenant and law given through Moses was to endure as the essential religious structure for the continuing community experience of Israel.

GOD AND THE NATION OF ISRAEL

Regardless of the problematic nature of the Exodus traditions, it is clear that this period was the crucible from which the new nation of Israel emerged. Not all at once, to be sure, for several centuries of trial by fire were to pass before the people of God could think of themselves as a nation "like all the nations" (I Sam. 8:5). In the Mosaic period the most we can discover in respect to nationhood, defined in terms of the characteristics of a typical politically organized state, is a confederation of originally independent, though ethnically related, tribes.

But was the first real unity of these tribes formed in Egypt, or in Sinai, or in Canaan? And did this unity stretch back to the time of Abraham, or was it newly created in or shortly after the Mosaic period? Whatever may be the answers to these and other questions regarding Israel as an emerging nation,[14] the essence of national unity for the Israelites was allegiance to one God, Yahweh. It was the covenant that held the Jacob-descended tribes together in a monolithic structure with Yahweh as head of the theocratic state or confederation.

In actuality, the loosely related tribes of Israel formed a rather fluid community, both in the time of Moses and in succeeding centuries. Clans and tribes departed or were added to the community on several occasions, depending ultimately on the degree of their willingness to abide by the terms of the covenant. But the ideal community, not always realized in fact, was the twelve-tribe amphictyony, an expression of religiopolitical unity not peculiar to Israel.[15] In Israel, however, this system provided whatever cohesion the tribes had from the time of Moses, or perhaps Joshua, to the time of David and even beyond.

It was Israel's view that such a system was created by the will of God. He had blessed and guided the fortunes of Jacob's sons through the dark days in Egypt, then out of bondage to a new life in a new land—their land by virtue of the promise to Abraham. We may say historically that the beginning of the nation Israel, and certainly the traditions that later gave cohesiveness to that nation, are to be seen in the time of Moses. The covenant-making God of Moses, indeed, the God of Abraham, Isaac, and Jacob also, was therefore the nation-making God of Israel both in the tribal period, when the nation was as yet incipient, and in the more structured monarchical period yet to come.

III

The Lord of Hosts: God and War

THE "BOOK OF THE WARS OF YAHWEH"

Any division of Old Testament history and literature into distinct periods runs into the problems of continuity and overlap. The era of Israel's exodus from Egypt and conquest of Canaan is really one discrete period, but we have chosen to separate the two phases of this period in order better to discuss the ideas about God which appear to dominate each phase. In addition, there is some justification for doing this in the material itself, since Moses is the leader during the exodus, while Joshua leads the conquest of the promised land. In any case, the understanding of Yahweh as a God of war is the controlling idea of the time of the conquest, and we shall see that the significance of this idea also extends beyond this one era alone.

Even before the days of the Israelite invasion of Canaan (ca. 1250–1200 B.C.)[1] Hebrew traditions of Yahweh's role in warfare had come into being. War and marching songs, or fragments thereof, were attributed to Miriam (Ex. 15:21) and to Moses (Ex. 15:1–18) in connection with the victorious crossing of the Red Sea (Ex., ch. 14). And other snatches of early battle slogans or songs are found in Ex. 17:16 and Num. 10:35–36; 21:27–30. The impression given by such fragments as these is that Israel had begun in the exodus period to view herself as a people marshaled by Yahweh to do battle according to his plan and purposes.

We may say, therefore, that the concept of Yahweh as God of war is an early one, that it had its focus in the time of Joshua and

the conquest of Canaan for obvious historical reasons, and that
the idea would necessarily impinge upon the subsequent growth
of Israel's understanding of God.

In a sense, every Old Testament writing that is concerned with
Yahweh's role in warfare belongs to the "Book of the Wars of
Yahweh." The Old Testament itself, however, uses this title for an
ancient collection of war poems and records, a small portion of
which is quoted in Num. 21:14 f. Unfortunately, we can say
nothing more about this ancient "book," for it is mentioned nowhere else in the Old Testament.[2] That there was such a collection
by this title at least indicates the origin and importance of the
God of war idea in premonarchical Israel.

Of even more importance for our study than the references in
Exodus and Numbers are the materials collected in the books of
Joshua and Judges. Much of this material is the product of later
writers (J and E) and editors (D), but, again, the judgment of
scholars is that apart from the obviously interpretative and didactic elements, these traditions genuinely reflect the history and
thought of the period they represent. In Joshua, the Israelite
forces under the leadership of Moses' successor began their military assault upon Canaan from across the Jordan River, and in a
series of mighty victories, mixed with only temporary setbacks.
Yahweh assisted his people in taking the land that had been
promised long ago to Abraham's descendants. In the process of
recording these events the writers, perhaps unwittingly, raised
some serious questions about the nature of the God of Israel,
questions that will be of central concern to our study in this
chapter. The Book of Judges also contributes to the development
of the idea of Yahweh as a God of war and to the view that
Israel's success in Canaan must be attributed almost entirely to
God's intervention at certain moments in history, particularly in
times of war, as well as to his Lordship over all of history.

YAHWEH SABAOTH

Before we turn to the accounts that illustrate the concept of the
God of war, it will be worthwhile to take up briefly the use of one

of the strongest appellatives applied to God in this connection,
Yahweh Sabaoth. This term is ordinarily translated "LORD of
Hosts" or "LORD of Armies," although the original meaning of the
Hebrew word *sebaot* is now indeterminable. Wherever it is used,
however, the context is invariably that of God and war. It has
sometimes been argued that in the later literature of the Old
Testament the word "Hosts" may refer to God's heavenly cohorts,
whose presence is suggested in a number of passages (Isa., ch. 6;
Job 1:6; 2:1; Ps. 24:10). But even in The Psalms we find that the
primary connotation of Yahweh Sabaoth is that of a God of war
whose power can bring about the defeat of the nations (e.g.,
Ps. 46).

Yahweh Sabaoth is not clearly associated with the time of
Moses. In Ex. 12:41, "all the hosts of the LORD" refers to the
people of Israel as they left Egypt. There is a similar reference to
"the ten thousand thousands of Israel" in Num. 10:36, which has
to do in part with battle, but the term *sebaot* is not used here.
The more explicit idea of the Israelite hosts as an army of God
seems to have its beginning in the time of Joshua.

There is a fragmentary story in Josh. 5:13–15 that tells of a
"man" who appeared before Joshua at Jericho and identified himself as "commander of the army (*seba'*) of the LORD." This "commander" directed Joshua only to remove his shoes, for he was
standing in a holy place, but the story was no doubt inserted at
this point because the account of the Israelite assault upon
Jericho immediately follows. A very important use of Yahweh
Sabaoth is found in I Sam. 17:45, where David said to Goliath:
"I come to you in the name of the LORD of hosts, the God of the
armies of Israel." The use of Yahweh Sabaoth in parallel with
"God of the armies of Israel" is undeniable evidence of the martial
aspect of God's nature in this period of Old Testament thought
(cf. also I Sam. 1:3).

Although references to the LORD of Hosts are not numerous,
they are at least suggestive of the military theme that runs through
the period under consideration, from Joshua to David. Even a
later spiritualizing of the idea of God's "hosts" does not lessen the
significance of the title "Yahweh Sabaoth" for the present period.

This significance will become even more evident as we turn now to the concept of holy war.

THE CONCEPT OF HOLY WAR

In the days when Yahweh was the local mountain deity of Midian it is doubtful that specific warlike characteristics were attributed to him, although we cannot be sure of this. The Midianite tribes were a wide-ranging nomadic people who attacked settled agricultural communities (see Judg., chs. 6 to 9), but, since most gods were localized among ancient Semitic peoples, it is probable that Yahweh remained on his holy mountain. With the coming of Israel, however, there was a transformation of the idea of Yahweh as a local god. Yahweh made a covenant with Israel, into which was incorporated the ancient promise of a land; he brought them out of Egypt "with a mighty hand"; and, as LORD of Hosts, he led them in the invasion and conquest of Canaan.

Thus it was in the exodus that Yahweh actually became Israel's war god. Their first great military victory was at the crossing of the Red Sea, celebrated in the militant songs of Moses and of Miriam:

> I will sing to the LORD, for he has
>   triumphed gloriously;
> the horse and his rider he has
>   thrown into the sea.
>
>   . . . . .
>
> The LORD is a man of war;
>   the LORD is his name.
>   (Ex. 15:1, 3.)

On the journey to Canaan, Israel fought unsuccessfully against Amalekites and Canaanites (Num., ch. 14) because the LORD was not with them, but with his help they defeated the Amorites (Num., ch. 21) and the Midianites (Num., ch. 31). With these beginnings, and the subsequent invasion of Canaan and lengthy wars of conquest and expansion, the development of a concept of holy war as God's method of fulfilling his promise to Israel is not surprising.

One of the most explicit statements concerning the idea of holy war is that attributed to Moses in Deut., ch. 20. This statement is probably a seventh-century interpretation of the conquest of Canaan, in the judgment of many scholars, utilizing more ancient traditions that genuinely reflect a pre-Deuteronomic understanding of God and war. In this understanding, Israel's warfare is holy because the LORD himself is with them, and the priests of Israel are to assure the people before each battle that the LORD will fight for them against their enemies, to give them the victory (Deut. 20:1, 4). Through Moses the LORD also gave instructions concerning the size of the army and the type of men who were to serve, the offering of terms of peace to a city wishing to surrender, and the requirement of complete destruction of a city that resisted.

This last-named stipulation and the accounts of its implementation, particularly in The Book of Joshua, have caused some concern on the part of later readers. The sacrificial ban imposed upon Canaanite cities makes Yahweh appear to be cruel and ruthless. In the concept of holy war, however, the purity of Israel's religious life was thought to depend upon the removal of all potentially corrupting influences, especially in the new land where they were to settle. Moreover, the condemnation of a city (but not all living things in it; see Ex. 21:14) was looked upon as a holy sacrifice to God, an offering that would be pleasing to him.[3] In such ways the later writers were able not merely to justify what Israel had done, for they were not primarily interested in defending her actions, but to understand and interpret these events as divinely guided concomitants of holy war.

The wars of Yahweh aimed at the conquest of Canaan were further sanctified for the people of Israel through belief in the Promised Land idea. If God had promised this land to the heirs of Abraham as theirs alone, then the taking of it was no less than a sacred obligation as part of the divine plan of history.

GOD AND THE PROMISED LAND

An axiom of the theological view of history that colors the entire Old Testament is that the Land of Canaan (Palestine) was the special and exclusive property of God's chosen people. This view undoubtedly was the result of later reflection upon the events of Israel's past, especially upon the meaning of the exodus and the subsequent settlement in Canaan. We must assume, therefore, that the call of Abraham and the LORD's promises to him of a land, a people, and a blessing (Gen. 12:1–3) were interpretations of early happenings by historians whose faith was in large measure due to Israel's peculiar response to her past. It is such an interpretation that gives meaning and continuity to the books of the Hexateuch, namely, the understanding of promise and fulfillment.[4] Thus the books of Joshua and Judges, which describe Israel's conquest and consolidation of the Promised Land, must be read with this interpretation in mind.

The war of conquest and extermination as described in Joshua is, of course, holy war, as we have noted previously. It is sanctified because God so willed it and because he personally directed it. Probably the most outstanding single aspect of these accounts of Israel's battles is the emphasis upon Yahweh's presence with his people. He was so intimately involved in their struggles that he would give detailed instructions for besieging a city such as Jericho (Josh., ch. 6) or Ai (Josh., ch. 8), or he would throw hailstones down upon the enemy (Josh. 10:11), or cause the sun to stand still while Israel took vengeance upon her foes (Josh. 10:12–14). As the writer of Joshua repeatedly states, "The LORD God of Israel fought for Israel," and this was Israel's conviction from the earliest battles recorded in the Old Testament (Gen., ch. 14?) down to the Maccabean wars (I Maccabees) shortly before the beginning of the Christian era, and even beyond.

In this period, and continuing into the days of David (ca. 1000–961 B.C.), the presence of God among his people was assured by the appearance of the Ark of the Covenant.[5] The accounts in Joshua say little about the place of the Ark in ritual or worship, but its use in battle and in bringing to pass unusual events is notable on several occasions (Josh. 3:14–17; 6:8–11; cf. Num. 10:33, 35 f.; 14:44 f.). The belief in Yahweh as a God of war and the personalistic, nontranscendent view of his nature combined to make the Ark of the Covenant an especially potent symbol of his presence and power. We are not to think that Israel looked upon the Ark as somehow containing God or as being identical with God. Such a symbol, though sacred and in a real sense the locus of the numinous or holy, was nevertheless no more than a sign pointing to the reality behind it. The faith of Israel surely understood this, and thus, with certain exceptions to be sure, carefully avoided a confusion that could lead only to idolatry. The Second Commandment attempted to ensure against just such a confusion (Ex. 20:4–6).

Having led his people in the successful conquest of Canaan,[6] Yahweh then assisted them in getting settled in the land and in establishing their claims in the face of hostile and aggressive neighbors. The story of Yahweh as God of war, therefore, continues in the accounts in The Book of Judges that so dramatically illustrate the struggle of Israel to secure the land for her own possession.

GOD AGAINST THE GODS

The period of the Judges in Israel's history (ca. 1200–1020 B.C.) was one in which the Israelite tribes fought sporadically, and in most cases successfully, not only to retain their grasp on newly acquired territory, but also simply to prevent subjugation and extermination by enemies on all sides.[7] Again and again the people found themselves at the mercy of a stronger foe, and again and again the LORD acted to deliver them from their oppressors. So conscious was the historian in The Book of Judges of the relationship between Israel's situation in Canaan at a given point and her loyalty or disloyalty to Yahweh that he undertook to reconstruct the history of this period according to a cyclical pattern of events. In this pattern, outlined by the writer in Judg. 2:6 to 3:6, the people of Israel at certain times forsook Yahweh and worshiped the Baals and the Ashtoreth, who were localized Canaanite fertility gods and goddesses; the LORD then punished them by permitting their enemies to plunder and oppress them; and the LORD finally raised up judges to save them. After a time the same pattern would once more be repeated, and so it went throughout the time of the Judges.[8]

This patterning of history presupposes that Israel will prosper only when she is faithful to God within the covenant relationship, and that God acts in historical events. More specifically, in regard to the second presupposition, the LORD made himself known as leader in battle, on occasion punishing Israel in war, but more often directing the armies of Israel, inspiring military commanders, and helping in unusual ways to overthrow Israel's enemies. And we must understand that it was not vengeance that lay behind Yahweh's warfare in Judges, nor was it simply the wish to purify the land for his people; rather, it was the "jealousy" of the LORD that motivated whatever he did and that conditioned his relationship with Israel. This means that covenant loyalty or disloyalty was the primary factor determining the course of events, so far as Israel was concerned, during the period of the Judges. In other words, as we noted above, the struggle was essentially between God and the gods of other nations for Israel's highest loyalty.

We need not summarize here the exciting tales of such legendary heroes as Ehud, Deborah, Gideon, Jephthah, and Samson. The reader should review for himself the accounts of these men and women of God, who "judged" their people in the sense of bringing justice to them by delivering them from oppression, with the assistance of the LORD, and who held a position of leadership over the nation, or at least a portion of it, so long as they lived. One should note in these stories that the presence of the LORD is without exception the most important factor in the several military victories won by the various Israelite tribes in this period.

The Book of Judges does not add significantly to our understanding of Yahweh as God of war, although we discover that here he acts principally through an agent, "the angel of the LORD" (chs. 2:1, 4; 6:11 f.; 13:1-21) or "the Spirit of the LORD" (chs. 13:25; 14:6, 19; 15:14). In the case of the war against the Canaanites, however, Yahweh intervened directly to win a victory for Israel, one which was celebrated in the ancient and memorable Song of Deborah (Judg., ch. 5).[9] It is noteworthy also that the Ark of the Covenant had no really significant role in the wars of the period of the Judges.

DIVINE JUDGMENT THROUGH WAR

Throughout the period of the exodus from Egypt and the conquest of Canaan, and extending far into later history for that matter, the idea of God's judgment upon men and nations appears as an essential aspect of his involvement in war. We have already noted that the Judges of Israel were responsible for establishing justice in the land, and this they most often accomplished through the military defeat of Israel's opponents. Thus the judgment of God was understood to be present in the acts by which such heroes delivered their people from oppression and punished the oppressors.

The theological basis of the concept of divine judgment in the Old Testament is quite simple. Given the framework of the covenant relationship between God and Israel, it will be obvious that God was expected to be on Israel's side in every encounter, and that those who opposed Israel were therefore God's enemies too. When Israel won a military victory over her enemies, it was logically interpreted as a judgment of God upon wrongdoers. In these situations Israel was "right" and, conversely, her enemies were "wrong." On certain occasions Israel herself might be punished by God for some wrongdoing, as in the case of Achan's trespass at Ai in the time of Joshua (Josh., ch. 7), or when, because of her apostasy, the LORD gave Israel over to her oppressors in the days of the Judges. Such punishment was also divine judgment, but since this judgment did not permanently rupture the covenant, Israel could expect to regain the LORD's favor and protection upon the resumption of covenant loyalty. We shall see further in the age of the great prophets that Yahweh could even bring other nations to punish Israel for her sinful ways.

What we have said thus far about the theological basis of divine judgment assumes that an ethical consideration is necessarily involved also. We cannot understand what it means to speak of Israel as "right" and her enemies as "wrong" apart from an understanding of the ground of such statements. In the first place, the concept of justice in the Old Testament does not presuppose an absolute standard of ethics. We have already observed that Israel was not chosen by the LORD because she was any *better* than other peoples (above, pp. 55 f.), and in specific situations her behavior was little different from that of her neighbors. In the second place, right and wrong were not so much determined by actions as by relationships. An action that might appear to an objective observer as wrong, e.g., the wholesale destruction of a city, could be interpreted as right in view of the covenant relationship. It was right, not in any arbitrary sense, but as part of the overall plan of God in history. And, in the third place, the ethical basis of divine judgment was more concerned with forensic rights than with moral right. This means that the real concern was to make right, to rectify, whatever was wrong, where the standard for right and wrong was always that which God willed for his people.

It is to the credit of the Old Testament writers, historians as well as prophets and poets, that the divine judgment was never seen as partial. Justice was absolute in the sense that it applied equally to the people of God and to other nations, and Israel was to suffer the divine punishment on many occasions. Nor was this view of God's judgment through war confined to historical time and to immediate events. Although, strictly speaking, the idea of a final great cosmic battle belongs to the later period of the prophets, it is appropriate to conclude this chapter with a brief preview of the concept of eschatological war.

THE ESCHATOLOGICAL WAR

Since Yahweh was in Israel's view the supreme Lord of history who, as we have emphasized in this chapter, frequently through war controlled the destiny of his people, it is not surprising that the idea of a final denouement in time should be pictured as a great cosmic battle. Such a picture was sketched in by several of the eighth- and seventh-century prophets of Israel (see Chs. VI and VII below), sometimes in historical terms, but more often in apocalyptic terms. The idea is that at the end of present time the forces of evil will be confronted by the forces of good, i.e., the people of God, in a last great battle in which God will finally triumph.

The Old Testament conceptions of judgment and punishment usually accompany these apocalyptic pictures of the end-time. The Day of Judgment or the Last Judgment almost always is expressed as a day of victory for God's people over their enemies —a day when "all the nations" shall finally come to acknowledge the sovereignty of God. But in the Final Judgment the righteous are to receive their reward, and the wicked who have opposed the Lord are to be punished.

The eschatological war comes as the climax of all sinful opposition to God. It is not that God planned it to be this way, but that the powers of evil have in actuality forced his hand. The prophet Ezekiel symbolically described the great battle as beginning with the aggressive attack of Gog, symbol of all enemy forces, against peaceful Israel. In the cataclysmic struggle that is to follow, God himself will participate in "jealousy" and "blazing wrath" to defeat the hosts of evil. He will summon the forces of nature against Gog, using earthquake, pestilence, torrential rains and hailstones, fire and brimstone, to destroy him completely— actions that are identified with God's entering into judgment against evil (Ezek. 38:21 f.).

Thus we see that to the end of time God is involved with war as a way of bringing to pass his holy will. This is not to say, from the Biblical point of view, that he wishes to destroy and to wreak havoc in order to express his will. His overriding concern is that his greatness and holiness be shown and that nations will know that he is the Lord. But to this end, whenever necessary, God may use war as a means for the accomplishment of a greater good for his people and for his world.

IV

God and Kingship

GOD AS KING

In the preceding chapters we have remarked more than once upon the unique qualities of God's relationship with his people, Israel. They saw him as Creator, as God Most High (El Elyon), as Lord of history, and as One who elected Israel, bound himself to her in the covenant, and repeatedly acted in history to guide, judge, punish, and save her. In a profoundly significant way, Yahweh was the only God for Israel, and it was inevitable in the ancient Near Eastern milieu that Israel should come to think of her sovereign Lord as King.

The idea of God as King was, of course, not confined to any one period of Israel's thought. It was not apparently an important idea in the premonarchical period, and many authorities believe that the kingship of Yahweh arose as an extension of ideas about the human king. We have chosen, therefore, to discuss the subject of God as King at this point in our survey of Old Testament thought because of its association with the beginning of kingship in Israel, recognizing that the conception itself extends far beyond this period and, indeed, finds what is perhaps its highest expression in rather late Old Testament usage and in the New Testament.

The institution of royalty was a most natural model for an ancient people to express the idea of their deity's rulership. In Egypt this idea took the form of divine kingship, i.e., the earthly king was the god incarnate, so that there was less emphasis upon the god (or gods) as the heavenly ruler. In Mesopotamia the human ruler was ordinarily thought to possess divine qualities and to rule as the earthly representative of the heavenly power. Thus, in both cases, the sovereignty of the deity was expressed essentially in the special relationship he had with the human ruler.

Israel chose neither of these two paths in her understanding of God as King, although the early kings of Israel were thought to have had a special relationship with God. As we shall see in the next section, there was usually a tension, rather than a complete identification, between Yahweh and the kings of Israel. The Old Testament provides for us a picture of Israel's efforts to preserve the majesty, dominion, and power of God for him alone, not to be shared with an earthly surrogate. And it may be that in the attempts to make Yahweh the only God for Israel, one of the most effective means was the notion of his sole sovereignty.

It is the later Old Testament writers, in the prophetic books and in Psalms, who speak most explicitly about God as King. We should not expect that pre-Davidic Israel would think very kindly of monarchy as a model for God's position of authority, both because of bitter experience with human rulers, as in Egypt, and because of lack of experience with a kingship of their own. And even when a kingship was established in Israel, at least one faction remained strongly opposed to it on the ground that Yahweh alone was to be their ruler (I Sam. 8:4–7; 10:19; 12:12, 19 f.; cf. Judg. 8:22 f.). We find, however, that as the monarchy came gradually to be accepted, the kingship of God was heightened rather than obscured. This was in large measure due to a spiritualizing of the concept by the later writers, who tended to idealize the theocratic state, projecting it into a future end-time, and who at the same time began to transform the human ruler into a more than human Messiah. The psalmists, for example, hardly ever speak of God as King in other than a glorified sense; he is "King over the whole earth," "a great King above all gods," and so on. And even the prophets, with their keen appreciation of the meaning of history, tend to describe God's kingship in its eternal and universal, rather than historical and concrete, sense. We shall return to such conceptions later in this chapter, having thus far attempted only to introduce the subject of God as King.

GOD AND KINGSHIP IN ISRAEL

The concept of kingship in Israel is of considerable interest in relation to the idea of God as King. In the first place, the introduction of the monarchy came at a time of serious historical crisis for the confederated tribes of Israel. The monarchy was traditionally instituted by God in response to the crisis posed by the threat of Philistine domination of the Israelite tribes, but in turn the monarchy itself was thought by some to be a serious threat to the theocratic way of life under God within the confederacy. Thus, in the second place, a theological crisis was involved in the very real historical problem that the people faced. There can be no doubt that this crisis was articulated by some groups at the beginning of the monarchy, although it probably did not take written form until a few generations later.[1] And a third factor to be considered is that of the reciprocal influences of Israel's thoughts about God as King, on the one hand, and about the king as God's agent, on the other hand.

What does the Old Testament concept of kingship tell us about the understanding of God as King? According to the sources in First Samuel, Israel's first kings were chosen by Yahweh himself and endowed with the power of his Spirit (e.g., chs. 10:1, 6, 10; 16:13). These men were charismatic rulers who, like the judges before them, often acted under the impulse of the divine power and grace. Moreover, the king held such titles as Anointed (Messiah) of Yahweh, Chosen One, and Son, in all of which we are to see not only the elevated stature of the earthly ruler, but also the majesty of the divine ruler and the strength of his own righteous rule.

The human king, as God's chosen one, was the visible representative of the invisible King. He was the instrument by which Yahweh exercised government over his people, and his office was not merely by God's grace; it was also in God's stead. He represented the kingship of Yahweh by holding a generally accepted position in the theocratic state as Yahweh's vicegerent. As such, he represented God before the people and the people before God, but neither God nor people were obligated to go through him as sole channel to the other, and thus he was not considered an indispensable mediator. Election and covenant between Yahweh and Israel was an established fact long before the beginning of the monarchy, and, despite the special covenant with the house of David (II Sam. 7:18–29), the king simply had to fit into that relationship.

In theory the Hebrew monarchy was theocratically based, with God at the center of the human kingdom and no real incompatibility existing between the sovereignty of Yahweh and the power of the human king. But there was nevertheless a factor of tension between the heavenly and the earthly ruler, a tension that is evident in all the Old Testament accounts, from Saul to the last king of Judah. Hardly a ruler in the long history of Israel's monarchy was to escape some touch of prophetic denunciation, and many of them were condemned outright. The very establishment of a human kingship had seemed to some an unmistakable descent from the lofty ideal of the theocracy, a materializing and externalizing of the divine rule. And this suspicion seemed confirmed on more than one occasion when the reign of a king was so unlike the ideal of the divine rule that it was impossible for the people to identify his rule with that of the LORD.

The picture of Yahweh as a gracious sovereign was in no sense marred by the imperfections of the historical monarchy or by its far from perfect representatives. In the historical writings Yahweh's sovereignty was never challenged without a response suitable to the challenge. He was never discouraged or swayed from his purposes by the failures and vicissitudes of his earthly agents. He remained loyal to the covenant, dispensing judgment as either reward or punishment according to the situation, and ever seeking to redeem and to restore his wayward people. The majesty and power of God simply became more awesome and more assured in the thought of Israel by the effects of the course of history. Indeed, the concepts of the Kingdom of God and of God's rule over the people, the nations, and the universe seem to have developed largely out of Israel's very real experience of God as Lord of history.

THE KINGDOM OF GOD

Israel's theocratic ideal was never fully realized in history. The Kingdoms of Israel and Judah could never have been mistaken for the Kingdom of God, and as time passed, the earthly ruler seemed less and less like his heavenly counterpart. And even though at times priests and prophets played a major role in national affairs, the monarchy was for the most part a thoroughly secular institution with essentially secular interests. To be sure, God was still nominally the head of this desacralized state, but his Lordship, vis-à-vis the political realm at least, came increasingly to be a matter of formality. There is convincing evidence in the Old Testament records, for example, that Yahweh was annually proclaimed King as the highlight of rituals celebrating the New Year,[2] one of the most significant of ancient Israelite festivals. Beyond this ritual observance, however, it appears that the kingship of God meant little in the daily routine of the nation.

In the midst of this concrete historical situation it is amazing that the Old Testament writers did not lose sight of the central tenet of God's sovereignty. The prophets, priests, and psalmists who are responsible for much of the literature of the Old Testament were always aware that the kingdom in which they lived prospered or suffered only because of the sometimes mysterious purposes of God. The divine King continued to rule, even when his Lordship was apparently denied by the attitude and acts of the national ruler, for the sovereignty of God was manifested for all who would see it in the events of history—events that transpired regardless of human plans and actions. Thus it was eventually only in a spiritual sense, in a manner transcending historical limitations, that the Kingdom of God could be conceptualized by the Old Testament writers. This is not to say that the Kingdom was ever so conceptualized in ancient Israel, for the Old Testament references that give substance to an idea that we call "the Kingdom of God" have certainly not been systematically formulated. From such references we can only infer what the Old Testament writers may have thought about the Kingdom of God, if indeed they thought about it at all.

What can be said, then, about the Old Testament idea of the Kingdom of God? We have already observed that the Kingdom is not to be identified with the earthly realm, although God certainly rules there too, and that the basis and essence of the Kingdom idea is simply that God is King. Most of the Old Testament passages that speak of the Kingdom of God have in mind his sovereign rule of all things, from the individual to the universe itself. The term "Kingdom of God," however, is *not* used in the Old Testament, a fact that serves to point up the nonspeculative, action-oriented nature of Old Testament thought. Instead, there are many references to God's "dominion," "reign," "sovereignty," or "kingship."

> For dominion belongs to the LORD,
> and he rules over the nations.
> (Ps. 22:28.)

> The LORD reigns; let the earth rejoice;
> let the many coastlands be glad!
> (Ps. 97:1.)

Or, in I Chron. 29:11: "Thine, O LORD, is the greatness, and the power, and the glory, and the victory, and the majesty; for all that is in the heavens and in the earth is thine; thine is the kingdom, O LORD, and thou art exalted as head above all."

Most such references to God's royal majesty and power come out of the later "theology" of postexilic times.[3] There was a tendency in the later Old Testament writings to spiritualize ideas like that of the Kingdom of God, in part because of the frustrations of history in Israel's experience, and thus the reality of the Kingdom came more and more to be identified with accepting the authority of God in one's personal life, as was clearly the case with Jesus' teaching about the Kingdom. We will want to see how this understanding was expressed in the Old Testament before going on to consider the implications of God's kingship for the nations and for the universe.

GOD'S RULE OVER THE PEOPLE

Everything in the Old Testament perspective on the relationship between God and man presupposes God's authority over man—first over his people Israel, and then eventually over the entire universe. We have discovered already that his Lordship is bound up in the ideas of creation, covenant, judgment, and kingship, and these ideas do not begin to exhaust the total range of possibilities in the understanding of God's rule over man. For Israel, however, it was necessary to interpret God's rule in personal, immediate, historical terms, for this was ultimately the only way she could experience and understand the ways of God.

Israel's self-consciousness in relation to God, so far as we can determine from the Old Testament, was largely a matter of corporate identity, of identity with the community, tribe, or nation. Individualism is peculiarly lacking in most of the Old Testament, even when we take seriously the impact of such towering personalities as Abraham, Moses, David, Isaiah, and others. These men naturally stood out, but they saw themselves, and were seen, primarily as representatives of the people before God, not as unique individuals. In every case of an outstanding individual in Israel's history there is the deep sense of that individual's responsibility as a mediator between God and the people. Even the most reclusive prophets, such as Amos and Elijah, were significant not for what they did in their solitariness, but for what they did at the very nexus of the divine-human encounter. Only when the covenant community seemed to have reached its end as a historical entity in the dark days of Babylonian exile did a few voices begin to suggest tentatively a more individualistic relationship between God and his people.[4]

Despite this lack of emphasis upon the individual, there are frequent expressions of a personal experience with God's rule on the part of individuals in the Old Testament. We need not review the stories about and words of such men as Abraham, Jacob, Moses, Samuel, and the many kings, prophets, and psalmists who had such experiences, in order to make this point.[5] But one can see, for example, in the lives of almost all the Israelite kings, that an awareness of God's presence as King was kept before them either by their own consciousness or by the pronouncements of the ever-present prophets. While the prophetic evaluation of each king's reign in First and Second Kings is the result of later reflection upon the meaning of history, there is no reason to doubt that prophetic voices were raised in the king's own hearing during his lifetime. Invariably these voices judged the king on the basis of his loyalty to the higher authority of God.

It is in Psalms, however, that we find the most personal expressions of confidence in the rule of God. Some of the relevant psalms are individual prayers for deliverance:

> Hearken to the sound of my cry,
>   my King and my God,
>   for to thee do I pray.
>   (Ps. 5:2.)

> Thou art my King and my God,
>   who ordainest victories for Jacob.
>   (Ps. 44:4.)

Other psalms simply praise the rulership of God in lofty terms:

> Yet God my King is from of old,
>   working salvation in the midst of the earth.
>   (Ps. 74:12.)

> I will extol thee, my God and King,
>   and bless thy name for ever and ever.
>   (Ps. 145:1.)

In addition, there are several "enthronement psalms,"[6] probably used in the New Year rituals mentioned previously, in which the worshiping assembly acknowledged God as King. Presumably the Temple priest led the people in singing these hymns, which typically begin with a phrase like, "The LORD reigns." In these and other ways the people, in community and as individuals, were reminded of the reality of God's kingship over their lives.

GOD'S RULE OVER THE NATIONS

What has been said thus far in this chapter about the kingship of God has applied almost exclusively to the people of Israel.

From their point of view Yahweh was King over the nation of Israel, and even though as Lord of history he might determine the course of other nations, the belief that he was also King of the nations has not yet been clearly affirmed. Again we find this more far-reaching understanding of God's sovereignty for the most part in the later poetry and prophecy of the Old Testament.

It is important to note, however, the germ of this wider understanding in the literature of the period of Israel's monarchy. It does not matter that the editorial perspective of this literature is not contemporaneous with the time that it describes, for the substance of the material consists of extracts from the royal chronicles of the monarchy.[7] A passage like I Kings 5:7 tells us that Hiram, king of Tyre, said to Solomon, "Blessed be the LORD this day, who has given to David a wise son to be over this great people." That a foreign king ever made such a statement is doubtful, but the point is that it tells us something of what an *Israelite* writer believed concerning the authority of Yahweh over other nations.[8]

Throughout the historical accounts in the Old Testament we are impressed by the way in which Yahweh used other nations to carry out his purposes. This interpretation of events controls most of the narrative of the monarchical period, but it is not followed systematically or exclusively. Nothing is said, for example, to indicate that the LORD brought the king of Egypt up against Jerusalem (ca. 935 B.C.) to take away the royal and Temple treasures (I Kings 14:25–28). But compare with this the more typical treatment of the accounts of the Assyrian invasions of Israel and Judah during the reign of Hezekiah (II Kings, chs. 18 and 19). Israel's defeat by the Assyrians is specifically attributed to their breaking of the covenant, and Jerusalem was spared destruction only when the LORD sent his "angel" to ravage the Assyrian camp. Thus the Israelite historians saw the power of God to control other nations, without yet coming to the view that these peoples were ready to acknowledge his sovereignty.

The nations never did accept the rule of Yahweh during Israel's history, of course, but the hope and assurance that they would do so was frequently voiced by the psalmists and prophets.

At times this hope was more a desire for the LORD to punish the nations who had afflicted Israel (as in Isa. 11:11–16; 33:1–24; Jer. 10:25; 30:10 f.) than a wish that all nations should serve the LORD. Yet, according to Ezek., ch. 36, judgment upon the nations and Israel's subsequent restoration would serve both to vindicate the holiness of the LORD's name and to show the nations that the LORD indeed was God. Beyond this, the psalmists pray confidently that the nations may know and praise the God of Israel (Ps. 67), and they summon all nations to praise the LORD and to acknowledge his kingship (Ps. 96:7–13; 99:1; 100:1).

In the later literature of the Old Testament the understanding of God's rule over the nations is distinctively futuristic and eschatological. The Israelites had suffered too much in history to think that Yahweh would be accepted as King by all men in this world. The kingdoms of this world were not the Kingdom of God, and the hope for such a transformation eventually came to rest in the expectations of a new age when God would enjoy universal dominion.

GOD'S RULE OVER THE UNIVERSE

What we may call the concept of God's universal sovereignty is actually a compound of thoughts about the Kingdom of God, the coming of a Messiah, the eschatological Day of Judgment, and the beginning of a realm of justice, peace, and prosperity. Only a belief in the all-encompassing power of God to actualize these dreams could have sustained Israel's hope for such a future "Day of the LORD." Circumstances may well have required the prophets and poets of Israel to look so far ahead in order to find a basis for comfort and assurance, but this in no way detracts from the grandeur of what they envisioned. To see Yahweh as ruler over the entire universe was to see in him the fulfillment of Israel's most lofty expectations for her God and for herself. Anything less than this would surely have meant that Yahweh was not God.

God's rule over the universe is expressed in the proclamation of the future Kingdom by most of the Old Testament prophets.

In the preceding section we stressed the importance of the prophetic hope that all nations would turn to Yahweh, if not in realized history, at least in the last days. Such an understanding of God's rule, however, is historically oriented and in general does not require that the idea of the Kingdom be universal and spiritual. It is one thing to hope that the several nations of the ancient Near East would acknowledge the sovereignty of Yahweh, politically as well as theologically, and quite another to predict that Yahweh is and will be recognized as universal sovereign. Both ideas may be similar in kind, as prophetic visions of the future, but they are quite different in degree.

Since the eschatological conceptions of the prophets will be discussed more fully in later chapters, we need here only summarize their views of the coming universal Kingdom. Most important is the prophetic proclamation that the consummation of God's Kingdom will be a time of new charisma for all his people. The Spirit of God will be abundantly given when the people come fully to realize that Yahweh is God (Joel 2:27–29). That Spirit will also be present in the person of God's royal servant, the Messiah, who will rule in behalf of God in the new age (Isa. 11:1–5). Furthermore, the entire people of God will be reestablished and renewed, as though the future Kingdom would begin with a new creation—a return to the beginning as the fulfillment of the end (Ezek. 37:1–14).

Great emphasis is placed upon the peace or well-being (Hebrew, *shalom*) of those who will dwell in God's future Kingdom. The full manifestation of this universal rule of God means the inauguration of a reign of justice and righteousness (Jer. 31:34). The physical welfare of mankind is not neglected either. Although the Kingdom may be spiritually conceived for the most part, there are many suggestions of material prosperity under the universal rule of God (Isa. 54:11 f.; 60:17; 65:20–23; Amos 9:13–15).

The universality of God's rule will have become evident from what has been said above and in the preceding sections of this chapter. It was no small thing for a people who had thought almost entirely in exclusive terms to arrive at such a view of the Kingdom of God. Nationalism and the idea of the chosen people were not easily put aside and, in truth, these ideas were never completely discarded in Israelite thought. Yet it is also true that the hope for the LORD's rule over all men and nations in a Kingdom of righteousness and love is a very real part of the Old Testament understanding of God.

V

God in the Early Prophetic View

There is no one period in the history of Israel's religious thought that may be specifically designated "the prophetic period." In our roughly chronological survey of the Old Testament understanding of God we have already had occasion to refer to significant prophetic ideas, and we shall have to do so again in what will follow. We may say, however, that the institution of Hebrew prophecy had its real beginning soon after the settlement in Canaan and continued well into the postexilic period, possibly as late as the fourth century B.C. But there were certain exceptions to these time limits, as we shall see. In the next three chapters our survey will concentrate upon the unique and profound contributions of the Old Testament prophets to our knowledge and understanding of God. Purely for the sake of convenience, we have divided the material under discussion into these three periods: the period of the early prophets (eleventh to ninth centuries); the period of the great prophets (eighth and seventh centuries); and the period of the later prophets (sixth and fifth centuries).

THE REVELATION OF GOD IN OLD TESTAMENT PROPHECY

In the Old Testament the revelation of God is not confined to his acts in history; God also spoke directly to his people, and especially through the agency of the prophets. The Hebrew word *nabi'*, which we translate "prophet," means something like "one who calls (or announces)," but it is the Greek word *prophētēs,* "one who speaks forth," that more nearly represents what we have come to understand as the essence of the prophetic vocation. Nevertheless, in the total Hebrew view these men who were called to be the agents of divine revelation were in a uniquely significant sense spokesmen for God.

The prophetic voice in ancient Israel thus became the medium par excellence for the communication of God's word. Whatever may have been the prophets' own self-consciousness concerning their peculiar gift, they were consistently aware that they spoke for an Other. "Thus says the LORD" is the clue to understanding the nature of prophetic utterance, and the prophets were careful to distinguish their own words from those which came from God. Any discussion of how these spokesmen heard the divine word, what sort of "inner ear" or special sensitivity they may have possessed, becomes purely academic in the face of their own conviction that God in very fact spoke to and through them.

We find the divine self-disclosure taking a number of different forms in Old Testament prophecy. There was sometimes a highly charismatic effect associated with the hearing of God's word, producing a prophetic ecstasy that frequently expressed itself in unusual behavior patterns. Such behavior was attributed to the spirit of God coming upon or seizing the individual, especially in the earlier stages of Israelite prophecy. When, for example, Saul had been anointed by the prophet Samuel, "the spirit of God came mightily upon him, and he prophesied among them" (I Sam. 10:10), thus provoking the question: "Is Saul also among the prophets?" We shall note in a later discussion how such prophets as Elijah, Elisha, and Micaiah manifested the experience of the divine presence and word.

The prophetic office seems to have attracted to itself quite unusual individuals for the most part, individuals who today would certainly be looked upon as "outsiders." They did not conform to the demands of society, whether expressed by king, priest, or people, but hearkened only to what they believed to be the voice of God. There is little to indicate that these men were in any way trained or prepared for their task; rather, as charismatic persons they responded to the divine word in their own individual ways. They felt compelled to speak, or as Amos was to put it:

> The Lord GOD has spoken;
> who can but prophesy?
> (Amos 3:8.)

Sometimes the prophets banded together in groups called "the sons of the prophets" (II Kings 2:3; cf. I Sam 10:5), which were apparently bands of disciples or followers of some outstanding prophet. We also read about groups of court prophets (I Kings, ch. 22; cf. Jer. 27:12–15), and there is much in the literature of the psalms to indicate that the later Temple worship employed cult prophets in the liturgy of petition and response. Israel's most out-standing and best-known prophets, however, are those individuals whose words have been recorded in the several prophetic books of the Old Testament.

We have said that prophetic revelation is a way of knowing about God, alongside the revelation of God in history. Actually, the two media of God's self-disclosure are inseparable. The proph-et's message is always related to his own historical context, and what he says as the LORD's spokesman is both what he hears in God's word and sees in God's acts in history. We may not violate that historical context, either by ignoring it or by separating the prophet's words out from it, if we are to understand the prophet's message. Our primary responsibility is thus to listen to what the prophet believed to be the word of God for his time, so that we may in turn appropriate the meaning of that word for our own existential situation.

YAHWISM AND CANAANITE BAALISM

The Israelite prophets of the eleventh to ninth centuries B.C. found themselves in an environment in which the fledgling faith based upon the uniqueness of Yahweh was threatened by a more ancient and firmly entrenched religion, the worship of the Canaanite Baal gods. This worship, grounded in man's experience with nature, suited very well the needs of an agricultural society, and as the Israelites made the transition from pastoral to agricultural life, Canaanite Baalism was bound to offer an attractive means of coping with many of the problems encountered in their new way of life in Canaan.

The high god of the Canaanite religion, well known from the Ras Shamra texts, was El, whose name appears also in several titles for deity in Genesis.[1] He was worshiped at all the important cultic centers of Canaan and Phoenicia as early as the time of the patriarchs, and he undoubtedly left his impression upon the early Hebrew conception of deity. The Canaanite pantheon also included El's consort Asherah, the various powerful gods called Baal, who played a more active role in Canaanite mythology than El, and other female personifications such as Anath and Ashtoreth. All of these deities were nature or fertility figures, whose role, regularly imitated in Canaanite ritual, was to ensure the fecundity and productivity of all things. We may be sure that Israel in Canaan adopted some of these ideas and practices,[2] and, but for the prophets, Yahwism might eventually have merged with Canaanite Baalism. There were, however, fundamental differences between the nature of Yahweh and that of the Baals, and these differences must not be overlooked.

In the first place, Yahweh was almost always thought of in personal terms, as we have noted before. He entered into direct relationship with individuals and was known to them in personal encounter. In the mythology of Canaan the abode of the gods was in the heavens and they had little to do in daily intercourse with the affairs of man on earth. Secondly, the God of Israel was not localized, although he was frequently associated with certain sacred places. He was with his people in their travels as nomads and appeared to them in many different places. Among the Canaanites each region, village, or shrine worshiped a particular Baal god who was resident in that place and whose authority was thought to be limited geographically. A third difference is seen in the Old Testament view of God as one who related himself in a special way to a chosen group, usually the tribe in patriarchal times, but the people of Israel in later times. The covenant relationship depicted in Exodus, for example, is totally foreign to the religion of the peoples of ancient Canaan. The fourth significant difference is in the place of the deity in nature. We have discussed before the Old Testament idea of God as Creator and Lord of nature; he was never subject to nor part of the forces and processes of nature. But the Canaanites and most other ancient peoples found their gods in nature and believed that integration with nature was the primary blessing to be afforded by the worship of those gods. Finally, the Israelites came to see God also as Lord of history, who intervened from time to time on behalf of his people and for his own purposes. Thus they tended to view history in a linear manner, as opposed to the cyclical-natural view of events among other ancient peoples.

What we must try to discover now is what answer the early prophets had to give to the challenge of Canaanite religious thought and practice. What was there in Yahwism that led prophets such as Elijah and Elisha to stand alone against the power of Baal and his prophets?

ELIJAH, ELISHA, AND THE ZEAL OF THE LORD

By the middle of the tenth century B.C. the Kingdoms of Israel and Judah had become established as small but flourishing nation-states in the eastern Mediterranean political mélange. Northern Israel[3] in particular had found its place among the surrounding minor kingdoms, and in the process seems to have accommodated itself at several points to the somewhat common culture of those kingdoms. The most critical single point of such accommodation was of course that of religion. In the reign of Ahab (869–850) external religious and political influence reached a peak through the influence of the Phoenician princess Jezebel, whom Ahab had taken as his queen. It was her overzealous efforts to establish her native Tyrian Baalism as Northern Israel's official religion that provoked one of the most notorious episodes in the entire religious history of the Old Testament, and which called forth the prophets Elijah and Elisha.

The challenge to Yahweh offered by the Baal gods, as we have noted, was essentially that of the claim to control over nature. Belief in Yahweh had no doubt included such a claim also, but not in the pragmatic, down-to-earth manner found in Baal worship. The sex and fertility rites indigenous to Baalism had no place in a Yahwism fresh from the austerities of a nomadic desert existence.

When, therefore, the importation of Baal priests, prophets, shrines, and cultus was understood as the grave threat to Israelite Yahwism that it surely was, the response had to come from the zeal of Yahweh himself, expressed through the agency of his prophets. Elijah first took up the challenge by his direct attacks upon Ahab and Jezebel.[4] Elijah's concern was to show all Israel that Yahweh was God, not Baal. And in order to do this he had to demonstrate somehow that it was Yahweh, not Baal, who effectively controlled the forces of nature. He chose to do this, according to the Old Testament traditions, by a dramatic contest on Mt. Carmel between the power of Yahweh and the power of Baal. The fascinating account of this great hierophantic struggle, with its miraculous climax coming when the LORD sent down fire from heaven and then caused a drought-ending rain to fall, is one of the highlights of Old Testament narration (I Kings, ch. 18). Elijah thus achieved, in part at least, the result that he sought, for at the conclusion of this event all the people cried out, "The LORD, he is God; the LORD, he is God."

But the struggle was far from over, and when Elijah departed this world (II Kings 2:11), his work was taken up by his disciple Elisha, a leader of the sons of the prophets (II Kings 2:15). And again it was the zeal or spirit of the LORD that enabled these men to stand against the royal house and to demand that Yahweh alone be acknowledged as Israel's God. Elisha's success is to be seen in the bloody revolt of Jehu, instigated by the prophet himself, that virtually eradicated the dynasty of Ahab and Jezebel, including even some members of the royal family in the Southern Kingdom of Judah (II Kings, chs. 9 to 11). Whatever we may think of this method of reinforcing the claims of Yahweh's sovereignty, to the Old Testament historians it was a legitimate case of Yahweh's zeal prevailing over those who would have accepted the Baal as Israel's god.

In this period, therefore, we must understand that Yahweh was in a sense fighting for his life. For the prophets, it was Yahweh versus the gods of other nations, and only the rightness of their cause could have provided them with the strength to uphold faith in the LORD. Had they not done so, the distinctive aspects of Yahweh religion would almost surely have disappeared under the pressures of the popular nature religion that impinged upon it from almost all sides.

IMPLICATIONS OF APOSTASY AND SYNCRETISM

Elijah and Elisha had seen clearly the nature of the threat to Yahweh faith. As prophets of the LORD their duty was to speak on his behalf, and in many instances to act on his behalf, where action spoke louder than words. Therefore, they fought Baalism both in the religious and in the political arenas, which were not so widely separated in Hebrew thought and practice as we are accustomed to today.

The early prophets were well aware of the dangers to Yahwism in the twin threats of apostasy and syncretism. Any turning away from the total demands of loyalty to Yahweh was considered to be apostasy. Indeed, all the prophets were most inflexible and uncompromising on this point, so much so that we can again speak of an "implicit monotheism" in the prophetic attitude. Yahweh was still for them the "jealous" God. The prophets knew also that any turning away from Yahweh would inevitably mean an acceptance of some aspects of Baalism and eventually an identification of the functions, if not the very beings, of Yahweh and Baal. Such syncretism would thus have serious implications for Israel's religious and political existence.

Since Yahwism could not tolerate any other gods besides Yahweh, to acknowledge the Baal in any way whatsoever would weaken the fabric of Yahwism and lead eventually to the breakdown of the covenant relationship. It was bad enough for a private citizen to turn to other gods, but when the heads of state, representing the entire nation, accepted or even merely tolerated the alien practices, real disaster could only be the result. In the light of this concern we can better appreciate the intense zeal of prophets such as Ahijah, Elijah, and Elisha. The Old Testament writers who collected and edited the traditions from this period were highly sensitive to the problems of national apostasy, and they have left us a record that is absolutely clear about what happens when a nation denies the God who created and sustained it.[5]

Although the religious and political life of Israel are hardly separable, we can observe certain specific political implications for the Northern Kingdom growing out of any tendency toward apostasy and syncretism. The particular god that a nation acknowledges becomes not only the protector and benefactor of that nation, but also its sovereign and Lord. (Baal, for example, may mean "owner" as well as "lord.") In other words, Yahweh ruled over and possessed Israel as a nation—politically, geographically, and in every other way. Were this claim to be subverted by even a partial recognition of the authority of another god, the state would obviously be in danger of being taken over by the nation whose god they had come to recognize.

This possibility is not always clear in the political and military events of the eleventh through the ninth centuries, but in the case of Ahab and Jezebel there is no doubt that the propagation of Baal religion in the Northern Kingdom could have led to a Phoenician take-over. The mechanism of such a take-over had already been started, for the strong-willed Jezebel had brought in from Tyre at least four hundred and fifty prophets of Baal and four hundred prophets of Asherah (I Kings 18:19), had "killed the prophets of the LORD" (I Kings 18:13), and was altogether a much stronger person than the king Ahab. Jezebel's father, Ethbaal, was a priest who had usurped the throne of Phoenicia, and one who might well have jumped at the chance to seize power also in the neighboring Kingdom of Israel.

In any case, the possibility of external political control was inherent in religious apostasy and syncretism, and in later centuries such external control did indeed become a reality for both

Israel and Judah. The interpretation of such an eventuality by the Old Testament prophets and prophetic historians obviously will be consistent with what we have seen heretofore of their conviction that the people of the LORD can survive only when they remain the people of the LORD. Before turning to a fuller discussion of this interpretation, we must consider briefly the prophetic understanding of Yahweh's ethical nature in this period.

THE ETHICAL NATURE OF YAHWEH

From the earliest Hebrew traditions and writings we learn of the importance of ethical conduct to Old Testament religion. The concern for justice and righteousness among men, especially from Moses on, is a striking characteristic of almost every document in the Old Testament, whether it be law, narrative, history, prophecy, or poetry. And in contrast with the general standards of conduct among surrounding peoples, Israel's ideal was like a landmark in a confusing wilderness. Above all else, Israel's passion for high morality among men was due to her conception of a God who was himself a moral Being.

The prophets believed that Yahweh demanded righteousness because he was himself righteous. Other gods, in Mesopotamia, Syria-Palestine, and later Greece and Rome, were thought to be exempt from the moral code prescribed for men, but this was not the case in Yahwism. Just because Yahweh was essentially ethical, he could expect that his people behave in a manner consistent with his own nature. Thus the prophets, beginning with Moses,[6] denounced evils wherever they encountered them, among commoners and kings alike, and regularly renewed the demand that men live according to the ethical standards of the LORD. As we examine what these ethical demands were in the view of the early prophets, we shall look not so much for a particular code of conduct as for those principles which inform us more fully of the ethical nature of Yahweh himself.

One of the cardinal principles of Hebrew ethics was the requirement of obedience to God's will. In First Samuel two instances of the consequences of royal disobedience are reported. When King

Saul made an offering to Yahweh before a battle, the prophet Samuel interpreted his action as a violation of God's commandment and proclaimed that Saul's kingdom would therefore not be permitted by Yahweh to continue (ch. 13:8–15). Later, Saul's failure to sacrifice all the people and livestock of the Amalekites was likewise seen as a serious disobedience of God's will, leading Samuel to make the significant pronouncement: "Behold, to obey is better than sacrifice." (See I Sam., ch. 15, for the entire account of this incident.) Regardless of the anti-Saul bias of these narratives, the principle of obedience to God as a moral requirement is clearly expressed in the prophet's statements.

An even more pointed illustration of Yahweh's ethical demands is preserved in the story of David and Bathsheba. We must be careful not to permit any moralizing about the obvious sin of adultery in this affair to obscure the essence of God's righteousness as the basis of his requirement of human righteousness. David's adultery with Bathsheba was serious enough, but it must be remembered that this was only the superficial act which was symptomatic of his more deep-seated willingness to violate human rights. David had taken another man's property—Bathsheba was the wife of Uriah—and had then committed the worse evil of taking that man's life. But Yahweh, through the prophet Nathan, did not let David's crimes remain unnoticed or unchallenged. The story of Nathan's rebuke of David and David's subsequent admission of guilt (II Sam. 12:1–25) is another of the high points of Old Testament narrative art, and the clue to the real meaning of what David had done is found in the prophet's question: "Why have you despised the word of the Lord, to do what is evil in his sight?" (v. 9). The very nature of Yahweh could not tolerate such behavior among his people.

David was not the only Hebrew ruler who was deluded into thinking that he possessed "divine rights" that could trample upon certain basic human rights. Ahab and Jezebel also felt the wrath of the prophet Elijah on at least one occasion that had little to do with their more notorious sins of idolatry. This was the occasion of Ahab's desire to possess the vineyard of Naboth the Jezreelite (I Kings 21:1–29). Being unable to do so by legal means, Ahab permitted Jezebel to arrange for the execution of Naboth, on a false charge of blasphemy, then took possession of the vineyard. But the LORD sent Elijah to condemn these crimes, so reminiscent of David's, and to say in the name of the LORD that such evil would be punished by the destruction of the royal house of Ahab and by the violent death of Jezebel. The just God, who demands righteousness because he is righteous, here through the prophet pronounces judgment upon intolerable ethical behavior.

There are, of course, other examples of Yahweh's ethical nature, many of them associated with the prophetic opposition to Baalism and the evils involved in idol worship. We have given only a few selected examples of what God expects of his people because of what God himself is. The point is that God is ethical in his essence, not merely in his demands. It was thus that the prophets always understood him, as we shall see even more fully in the next chapter, when we come to the words and works of the great prophets of the eighth and seventh centuries.

THE "DEUTERONOMIC" UNDERSTANDING OF GOD

Much of what has been discussed in this and preceding chapters relates to what has been called the "Deuteronomic" point of view in Old Testament thought. Let us first look briefly at what is meant by this designation. In the opinion of most Old Testament scholars today the book of Deuteronomy was produced late in the seventh century B.C. by writers who had been greatly influenced by the prophets and who were deeply interested in the meaning of history. These prophetic historians also edited from earlier sources the books of Joshua, Judges, Samuel, and Kings, all of which are characterized by the so-called Deuteronomic outlook.[7] So significant was the prophetic spirit displayed by these works of history that in the Hebrew Bible they were called the "Former Prophets," while the books of the prophets Isaiah, Jeremiah, Ezekiel, and the Twelve (Hosea-Malachi) were designated "Latter Prophets."

We cannot speak of the Deuteronomic understanding of God

apart from the prophetic view of God and history. They are one and the same. There are two basic points to this prophetic or Deuteronomic understanding, both of which we have encountered before, and both of which are found consistently throughout the prophetic literature as well as the Deuteronomic histories. The first of these points is that Yahweh is the righteous God of history whose will is being carried out in all the events of historical time. This conviction had begun with the experience of Israel in the days of the exodus, and by the time of the great prophets it had expanded to include all nations as subject to the divine will and purpose of Yahweh. Illustrations of this first main point are abundant in Exodus, Deuteronomy, the Joshua-Kings collection, and all the prophetic books. The second point is that disloyalty to Yahweh, especially in apostasy and defection from the covenant, brings individual and national disaster and that true *chesed* or loyalty to Yahweh alone results in prosperity and peace or well-being (*shalom*) for people and for nation. Again, the illustrations of this conviction are numerous, particularly in Judges and Kings,[8] but throughout the prophetic literature as well.

The purpose of this rather severe judgment of history was not simply to criticize and condemn, even though many episodes in Israel's experience fully warranted condemnation. Rather, the prophetic analysis, not merely derived from historical events, but surely confirmed there, was designed to make past experiences edifying and to recall Israel to her God. In this connection it is important to remember that the "predictions" of the prophets were almost always *conditional;* that is, they warned that the people would be punished by Yahweh *unless* they returned from their evil ways to faith in Yahweh. The purpose was clearly to save, not to destroy, the people of God.

Thus the theological formula that characterizes the Deuteronomic view of God is central to the entire Old Testament, and to the entire Bible for that matter. Apart from the concept of Yahweh as the unique and only God, this understanding may fairly be said to be the single most important contribution of Israelite experience and thought to the Judeo-Christian understanding of God. In a very real sense, the First Commandment, "You shall have no other gods before me," can only be understood in the light of the prophetic-Deuteronomic view of God.

With this section we have reached a midpoint in our survey of the Old Testament understanding of God. The preceding chapters have largely been a look backward through the historical materials of the Old Testament, whereas now we are beginning to feel with the prophets a sense of the present and a looking forward to the future. To be sure, the prophets yet to be studied and the literature of cultus and of wisdom are also historically grounded, but we shall perhaps find in much of what follows a timelessness that was not so strongly felt in respect to the earlier materials. This perspective on the Old Testament may very well be purely subjective on the writer's part, and he freely admits it. It remains, therefore, for the reader to form his own judgment of whatever movement or dynamic of thought he may apprehend in this sketch of Old Testament theology.

VI

The Great Prophets Speak for God

MAJOR THEMES IN OLD TESTAMENT PROPHECY

It is possible to approach the message of the Old Testament prophets in a variety of ways, none of which would be either complete or satisfactory in every respect. No summary or outline of prophetic thought can possibly do justice to the rich diversity and depth of insight that we find in the books of the prophets, yet it will be useful at this point to discuss some of the major themes in Old Testament prophecy. We have already encountered a few of these themes, and most of those mentioned here will be taken up again later in this chapter and in the next. In this chapter we shall be concerned mostly with the words of the great eighth-century prophets Amos, Hosea, Isaiah, and Micah, and of two outstanding prophets from the last part of the seventh century and the early years of the sixth, Jeremiah and Ezekiel.[1]

The controlling idea of all Old Testament prophecy is the belief in the sole sovereignty of Yahweh. It is much more accurate still to use a term like "sole sovereignty" for the prophetic idea of God, since this term does not imply as much as "monotheism" would, yet it does say more than the limited term "henotheism"[2] would. In the next two sections of this chapter we shall take up this question again and shall attempt to arrive at some conclusions as to how the term monotheism may properly be used in this period of prophetic thought. For the moment it will be sufficient to remark that the prophets without exception uphold the covenantal concept that Yahweh alone is God for Israel. They condemn every aspect of idolatry, not so much on theoretical grounds as on the very concrete basis that recognition in any way of a god other than Yahweh breaks down the covenant relationship. The only legitimate avenue of approach to the sacred for Israel is through constant awareness, in both thought and practice, that Yahweh alone is King over all.

In the preceding chapter we observed that the early prophets of Israel had a keen sense of the ethical nature of Yahweh and of his requirements for human conduct. This is a second major theme in Old Testament prophecy, and it is one that we find most highly developed in the prophets of the eighth and seventh centuries. These men were intensely aware of the good and of the evil that they saw around them in human society. They could not remain silent when they witnessed personal immorality, social injustice, national corruption, disobedience to Yahweh, and all the other ills that were rampant among a people who were supposed to be living close to their God. Just because Israel was the privileged people of God, so would their failure to live according to his will be more severely punished, said the prophets. If the idea of Yahweh's sovereignty is the head of the prophetic understanding of God, then the concern for righteousness and social justice is the body and substance of their thought.

As the cultus of Yahweh developed and became formalized, especially after the building of the Jerusalem Temple by Solomon, the liturgy of worship and sacrifice seems to have become identified by the people with the essence and chief requirement of Israelite religion. But the prophets could not accept this identification, or rather, they could not tolerate the hypocrisy of Israel's ritualized worship of God which was so glaringly inconsistent with her moral response to God. The prophets did not object to the cultic observances per se—these had after all been central to Yahwism presumably since the days of Moses. They objected to the idea that true religion consisted solely of regular offerings and sacrifices, which for many undoubtedly had become meaningless habit. The prophets held that true religion was bound up with personal and moral obedience to the will of God. It could not be formalized in a prescribed set of actions to be performed on the Sabbath and at other special times. True religion was immediate, personal, and constant devotion to the holiness of God. We shall want to explore this prophetic theme a bit more in a later section of this chapter, as well as in Ch. VIII.

There are a number of significant ideas associated with the theme of God acting in history, a subject that has appeared throughout our survey. More broadly stated, this theme includes all the implications for history of the belief that Yahweh is Lord in the realm of human as well as of cosmic events. The past, present, and future are to be understood from the perspective of what Yahweh has done, is doing, and will do. For the prophets, there is no other way of looking at temporal existence, and even though such a view regarding Israel's life is normative in the Old Testament, the prophets expanded this concept to include everything in the whole time-space continuum, so far as they knew it. In particular, they held that all the nations surrounding Israel or having anything to do with her are subject along with the chosen people to the operation of the divine will in history. The implications of this world view for the Old Testament understanding of God are obviously of paramount significance.

Finally, we must give attention to the prophetic theme that concerns itself primarily with the future, aptly symbolized by the phrase, "The Day of the LORD." Included here are the ideas of the Day of Judgment (both punishment and reward), the victory of Yahweh over his (and Israel's) enemies, the appearance of a righteous ruler (the Messiah), the redemption and restoration of Israel, the establishment of a glorious kingdom of peace and prosperity, and the beginning of a new (timeless?) age for all mankind. As we shall see, prophecy becomes increasingly eschatological, that is, more and more involved with the coming end-time, and somewhat less concerned with temporal realities. Such a theme thus provides a remarkable climax for the prophetic understanding of God and his ways.

Our purpose in treating these major themes in Old Testament prophecy is simply to learn what they may teach us about a most important way of understanding God in the Old Testament—the prophetic way. The message of the prophets has, of course, high intrinsic value of itself, and we must not lose sight of that value in our efforts to learn what the prophets have to say about God. In effect, however, everything that the prophets have to say is in some sense a word about God.

MONOTHEISM—IMPLICIT OR EXPLICIT?

Did the prophets of the eighth and seventh centuries think and speak in terms of a monotheistic conception of God? This question can be answered only if we have a clear understanding of what is meant by monotheism. In discussing this subject earlier (Ch. II), we defined monotheism succinctly as "belief in the existence of only one God." The propositional language in which this definition is stated is, however, quite foreign to the Hebrews and to most other pre-Hellenistic peoples. The Old Testament writers, including the prophets, were not primarily interested in definitions and delimitations of concepts, but in pragmatic and experiential understanding or knowing. Therefore, in order to apply a term like "monotheism" to Hebrew thinking we must be acutely aware that the concept behind the term may be quite alien to that which is intrinsic to Hebrew thought. Or, to put it another way, the Old Testament understanding of God was probably never consciously monotheistic in an abstract sense, but was manifestly monotheistic in the sense that men were called to live for and to obey only one God, namely, Yahweh.

We may want to qualify this last statement somewhat as we examine the ideas of the Second Isaiah[3] in the next chapter. For the moment, however, we can assert that there is no explicit monotheism in Israel's history, so far as we know it from the Old Testament, until about the last half of the sixth century. The point we are attempting to make here has been cogently summed up by Millar Burrows: "The prophets before Second Isaiah may have had an implicit monotheism, either in the sense that they believed there was only one God but did not find occasion to say so, or in the sense that they held a conception of God that logically implied monotheism though they were not themselves fully aware of that implication. In the latter sense at least the faith of the eighth-century prophets was implicitly monotheistic. It was a practical, if not a theoretical monotheism, for their conviction that Yahweh controlled all nations and used them for his purposes, if carried to its logical conclusion, would—and later certainly did—lead to monotheism. Whether Amos and Isaiah and the rest saw this or not we cannot tell from what they say; at least they say nothing to the contrary."[4]

The central question of the nature and oneness of God has been of continuing interest in our study, whether formulated as the problem of monotheism or in some other way, and we shall continue to encounter it as we go along. As yet there is no definitive answer to the question, and such an answer is probably not to be expected, since we are dealing with the development of thought in the Old Testament, not with a static mass of words and ideas.

THE DEVELOPMENT OF ETHICAL MONOTHEISM

The consciousness of the moral nature of Yahweh that we have seen already present in the earlier prophets was a major contributing factor to the development of monotheism in the Old Testament. As the prophets reflected upon Israel's historical experience, their interpretation of events led directly to the conclusion that a righteous God was in command of all history. Such an interpretation, focused as it was upon a single ethical being, was instrumental in producing the distinctively prophetic notion of ethical monotheism.

Strangely enough, the eighth-century prophets first found this interpretation confirmed by Yahweh's judgment upon their own people in the form of national defeat. About the middle of the eighth century Amos of Tekoa pronounced harsh judgment upon Northern Israel, saying that her sins would lead to her downfall at the hands of Assyria (Amos 3:9-12; 5:1-7; 6:1-14; 9:7-10), a disaster that indeed took place with the fall of Samaria about 721 B.C. Hosea, too, concentrating upon Israel's idolatry, proclaimed Yahweh's grief over his people's unfaithfulness and unrighteousness, and spoke of Israel's punishment by foreign powers (Hos., chs. 4; 8; 13). The prophet Isaiah of Jerusalem was active during the years when the Northern Kingdom was being overrun and finally destroyed by Assyria, and in his message (i.e., Isa., chs. 1 to 39) there were many lessons for Judah drawn from Israel's misfortunes (see Isa. 9:8 to 10:4). Perhaps the most pointed of these lessons is that given by Isaiah in the sign of Immanuel, "God with us," as an attempt to prevent Judah, through its frightened King Ahaz, from giving up all trust in Yahweh in the face of national disaster (Isa. 7:1-25; cf. ch. 8:1-8). And Micah, a later contemporary of Isaiah, echoed the general denunciation of the whole people of Israel and predicted that Jerusalem would be destroyed just as wicked Samaria had been (Micah 6:9-16; cf. ch. 1:2-16).

The common element in these and many other prophetic passages having to do with the nation's distress is the conviction that Yahweh is at the center of all these events and that, for example, he not only uses a nation like Assyria to punish many kingdoms,[5] but also then destroys Assyria and uses the greater might of Babylonia for his further purposes. In other words, Yahweh's power over these nations is evidence for his superiority over their gods, and the logical conclusion, soon to be explicitly stated, is that the other so-called gods are really not gods at all. Yahweh alone is the ultimately moral being whose righteous will is revealed in what takes place on the stage of human events.

Thus the prophets declared again and again, often without specific intent to do so, the righteous nature of the Holy One of Israel.[6] The interpretation of history as a moral lesson, following the rubric of the "Deuteronomic school," which saw prosperity as God's reward for righteousness and obedience, and disaster as his punishment for wickedness and disobedience, resulted in the very special kind of Hebrew understanding of God called ethical monotheism. Other ways of speaking of Yahweh's being—as Creator of all things, Ruler of nature, LORD of Hosts, and King of Kings—which Israel had learned through her experience and reflection upon that experience, also contributed to the formula-

tion of this understanding of God. It was, however, the prophets'
stress upon the singleness of Yahweh's purpose, will, and being
that made it possible for Israel eventually to express consciously
an explicit or pure monotheism.

GOD AND THE SOCIAL ORDER

The ethical monotheism that resulted from the prophets' consciousness of the presence of Yahweh in all of Israel's experience
was effectively translated into an ideal for the social order. This
was done by the prophets, and by others in the Old Testament
for that matter, not at the level of abstraction but always at the
level of concrete human experience. Neither ethical monotheism
nor the social ideal was ever theoretically formulated by the
prophets. What they believed and said sprang inevitably from
their own confrontation with God in the everyday realities of their
social environment.

For the most part, the eighth- and seventh-century prophets
displayed a real disaffection for the citied and agricultural life
of their time. It seemed to them, as it did to the like-minded
"Deuteronomic" writers, that the days of Israel's greatest loyalty
to Yahweh lay in her nomadic past, before settlement in the Land
of Canaan had corrupted her in so many ways (e.g., Amos
5:25 f.). Earlier prophets such as Elijah and Elisha had expressed
a similar conviction, and even the latest editors and writers of the
Old Testament tended to glorify those days of supposedly greater
covenant faithfulness. It seemed to all these critics of Israel's
settled life that the wilderness was much more conducive to the
kind of trust in Yahweh and concern for one's neighbor that
ideally should characterize Israel as the people of God.

In regard to the social order, the prophetic ideal is beautifully
stated in a passage from Deut. 10:11–22 that is clearly part of the
same basic social thrust that motivated the prophets.[7] When in
vs. 12 f. we read: "And now, Israel, what does the LORD your God
require of you, but to fear the LORD your God, to walk in all his
ways, to love him, to serve the LORD your God with all your heart

and with all your soul, and to keep the commandments and statutes of the LORD, which I command you this day for your good?" we are immediately reminded of Micah's:

> He has showed you, O man, what is good;
>   and what does the LORD require of you
> but to do justice, and to love kindness,
>   and to walk humbly with your God?
>   (Micah 6:8.)

And the prophets would not permit the people of Israel to forget this ideal or to consider it a mere abstraction. They hammered away, both in public utterance and in private communication, on the numerous ills of Israelite society, on the standards that this society should live by, and on the penalties for failure to measure up to the requirements of being the people of God. Running throughout all of this is the awareness of what Yahweh had done for his people and of how his actions provided the basis for the structure of the social order. Thus the very real concerns of the prophets were grounded on their sensitivity to Yahweh's requirements and the failure of Israel to be the people of the LORD.

What were some of the specific concerns of the prophets in regard to the social order of their day? We cannot expect to find in the prophets a detailed constructive statement of what Israel's social order should be. The model was never drawn in other than general terms in the prophetic literature. What we do find is a rather complete catalog of the evils in Israelite society, along with exhortations to return to God's way lest his judgment fall heavily upon the nation.

Where the nation at its higher levels was concerned, the prophets did not exempt kings and others in authority from their criticism. The rulers of both Israel and Judah were guilty of such iniquities as land-grabbing (Hos. 5:10; Isa. 5:8; cf. I Kings, ch. 21), usurpation of the throne (Hos. 8:4), refusing to trust in the LORD (Isa. 7:10–17), misleading the people (Isa. 9:13–17; Jer. 23:1–8), making unholy alliances with other nations (Isa. 30:1–17; 31:1–3), and unspecified avaricious and irresponsible deeds

(Micah 3:1–4).[8] This selection does not exhaust the list by any means, but it is sufficient to indicate the kinds of problems that the prophets discovered at the royal level. The priests and court prophets were also frequently excoriated by the great prophets of this period, for these professional religionists had rejected the knowledge and teaching of Yahweh and were deeply sinful (Hos. 4:4–10; 5:1–2); they were unable to perform their duties because of drunkenness (Isa. 28:7–10; 29:9–12); they sought only their own mercenary gain (Micah 3:5–8, 11); and they falsely preached an easy popular message at the demand of the people (Micah 2:6; 3:5; Isa. 30:10; Jer. 5:31; 23:9–40; Ezek. 13:1–7).

The prophets indicted still others at a high level in Israelite society, namely, the judges, who perverted justice for a bribe (Amos 5:7; Micah 3:9, 11; Isa. 5:23), and the wealthy aristocracy, who selfishly thought nothing either of the poor or of the decline of their nation. In regard to the distribution of wealth, Northern Israel in particular seems to have had a rather inequitable situation. Only a few landowners and rulers were able to enjoy a comfortable, even luxurious, standard of living, while the great masses of the people lived meagerly, if not in abject poverty. The prophetic sense of social justice was upset by this unbalanced condition, and they were especially outraged at the excessive and ostentatious mode of living displayed by some of the most wealthy. Amos spoke in very strong language against such excesses and the lack of concern for the poor (chs. 2:6–8; 5:11; 6:1–7), the greed of merchants (ch. 8:4–6), and the self-indulgence of the rich women (ch. 4:1–3). The vain and wanton women of Jerusalem were similarly condemned by Isaiah in a harsh pronouncement that borders on bitterness (Isa. 3:16 to 4:1). Micah, too, was most vigorous in his attack upon the corruption of Jerusalem's upper class, their covetousness (ch. 2:1–2), deceit (ch. 6:9–12), and upon everything represented by the great cities of Jerusalem and Samaria (chs. 1:2 to 3:12).

All the above comments add up to the fact that, for the eighth-century prophets, the level of community morality in Israel and Judah was extremely low. In general their immorality consisted of violations of almost every provision of the Deuteronomic social ideal—the ideal of justice for the fatherless and the widow, love for the sojourner, care for the poor, and all the rest. The resulting social disorder is what the prophets criticized, and always with respect to real human rights and needs, for God's requirements of high morality were designed for a living community of people, not for some abstraction called the nation. In everything that the prophets had to say about the condition of Israel's society they never lost sight of the moral Being who as Israel's God required righteousness of his people and who promised to judge them and punish them for their sinful ways.[9]

GOD AND THE INDIVIDUAL

When we speak of the people of Israel, it is necessary to keep in mind that the community is made up of individuals. Although in the Old Testament the idea that "the state is the individual writ large" never really pertained, there was some sense of the importance of persons as individuals, and in some of the poets and prophets we find a developing idea of individualism. From the earliest times, however, the dominant mode of thinking among the Hebrews and other ancient Semitic peoples was that of collectivism. Most primitive peoples, in fact, have a much stronger sense of the group than of the individual person, and the group is frequently personified as an individual. This idea of "corporate personality" is an especially noteworthy aspect of Old Testament thought, from the early narratives about the patriarchs to the late poetry of the wisdom writers, and we shall need to consider it again when we come to the Second Isaiah and to the Wisdom Literature.

In the preceding chapter, as we noted the prophets' denunciation of the wickedness of Israel, we might have glimpsed something as well of the wickedness of individual Israelites. Those sinful acts which called forth the prophets' condemnation were after all committed by specific individuals in specific situations. Yet it is still necessary to translate the prophets' concerns from corporate to individual morality if we wish to discover any kind of personal ethical code. We simply do not find moral injunctions addressed to the individual as distinct from the community.

It is in the area of religious responsibility in the thinking of the Old Testament prophets that we first encounter an emphasis upon the individual apart from the community. Neither the early prophets nor the four major prophets of the eighth century had couched their proclamations in terms of individual responsibility to Yahweh; they always addressed themselves to the community, the class, or the nation. Whether they ever looked upon these groups as made up of individuals, or ever thought of singling out individuals as responsible for their own religious and moral conduct, we cannot say, since they are silent on this point. Apparently, these prophets thought and spoke almost entirely in the plural rather than in the singular. But in Jeremiah and Ezekiel, the two prophets who appeared toward the end of the period presently being discussed, we have the first hints of an awareness of the individual as a person identifiable within or even apart from the group. The historical conditioning that may have been largely responsible for this development was the decline and disappearance of the group—the nation of Judah in this case—in which individuals had heretofore largely found their identity. Thus the fall of Jerusalem in about 586 B.C. was a traumatic and epochal experience in Israel's history in more ways than one.

To be sure, Jeremiah and Ezekiel in most respects thought very much like all the other prophets of their time where the community was concerned. They too condemned the whole people of God on numerous counts, and their messages were directed to the community as such. At one point, however, these two prophets departed from the traditional view. The ancient belief in collective responsibility held that guilt involved the entire community or social group, especially the family.[10] But the seventh-century Deuteronomic reinterpretation argued that "the fathers shall not be put to death for the children, nor shall the children be put to death for the fathers; every man shall be put to death for his own sin" (Deut. 24:16). This principle of individual responsibility was also upheld by Jeremiah and Ezekiel. Jeremiah projected such responsibility into the eschatological future:

In those days they shall no longer say:
"The fathers have eaten sour grapes,
    and the children's teeth are set on edge."
But every one shall die for his own sin; each man who eats
sour grapes, his teeth shall be set on edge (Jer. 31:29–30).

Ezekiel, however, quoting the same ancient proverb and likewise
denying its validity, discussed the responsibility of the individual
in considerable detail as a present reality. He was primarily concerned with the idea as an extension of God's justice. The justice
of Yahweh demanded an individual, rather than corporate, approach to the problems of iniquity and righteousness, for in the
latter way the innocent too often suffered along with the guilty.
Although this principle was not further elaborated by the prophets, and does not loom large in their overall concerns, it does
indicate a shift of emphasis and a trend that was eventually to
become an important religious theme, notably in the New Testament.

WHAT DOES THE LORD REQUIRE?

Turning now to the prophets' analysis of the religious situation
in Israel, we find that they concentrated upon two main problems
in seventh- and eighth-century Yahwism. The first of these, noted
briefly at the beginning of this chapter, was the problem of the
hypocrisy of Israel's public religious ceremonies, divorced as they
were from what the prophets believed Yahweh actually desired
and required of his people. Prophetic religion would seem to be
something quite far removed from cultic religion, and in a real
sense a judgment upon the cultus. The second, and perhaps even
more important problem, was that of idolatry, which we have
observed as a continuing threat to Israel's covenantal faith since
the time of Moses. Since we have encountered this problem in one
form or another in every period of Old Testament history thus
far,[11] we shall only summarize at the end of this section what the
prophets from Amos to Ezekiel had to say about it.

The eighth-century prophets plainly felt that something was
terribly wrong with Israel's worship of Yahweh. Why would Amos
say:

> Come to Bethel, and transgress;
> to Gilgal, and multiply transgression
> (Amos 4:4.)

in reference to two of the Northern Kingdom's major cultic centers? And why did he understand the LORD to demand that the people seek him instead of seeking Bethel and Gilgal? (ch. 5:4 f.). The answer to these and similar questions on the prophet's attitude toward the cultus is to be found in his concept of ethical monotheism. Although Amos spoke in an extremely negative manner concerning religious rituals, offerings, and sacrifices (ch. 5:21–23), we have no reason to believe that he wished to eliminate the cultus completely.[12] But he could not stand to see such public displays of piosity when there was wickedness and rejection of Yahweh's ethical requirements on every hand. Therefore, Amos expressed the heart of his message in a brief but telling phrase at the conclusion of his criticism of cultic worship:

> But let justice roll down like waters,
> and righteousness like an ever-flowing stream.
> (Ch. 5:24.)

The moral requirement thus takes precedence over the ritual requirement, in all the prophets of this period as well as in Amos (cf. Isa. 1:10–17).

The call for righteousness, justice, covenant loyalty, and mercy is renewed in Hosea (ch. 2:19 f.), where also "steadfast love" and "the knowledge of God"[13] are to be preferred to sacrifice and burnt offerings (ch. 6:6). It was Micah, however, who proclaimed the most sweeping judgment upon the cultus, and who most eloquently spoke of the LORD's requirements. He first condemned the corruption of Judah's rulers, priests, and prophets, as we have seen, and then uttered the unprecedented prediction that Jerusalem and its Temple would be destroyed because of such corruption (ch. 3:9–12). Only Jeremiah a century later, of all the prophets, dared to make a similar assertion concerning the LORD's city and house (ch. 7:1–15; cf. ch. 26:1–19). But Micah is best known for his excellent poetic summary of the essential requirements of religion and of religious life:

"With what shall I come before the LORD,
    and bow myself before God on high?
Shall I come before him with burnt offerings,
    with calves a year old?
Will the LORD be pleased with thousands of rams,
    with ten thousands of rivers of oil?
Shall I give my first-born for my transgression,
    the fruit of my body for the sin of my soul?"
He has showed you, O man, what is good;
    and what does the LORD require of you
but to do justice, and to love kindness,
    and to walk humbly with your God?

(Ch. 6:6–8.)

Jeremiah's Temple sermon (ch. 7:1–15) and Ezekiel's later description of the LORD's glory leaving his Temple (ch. 10:1–22) add significant weight to the prophetic critique of the cultus and cultic worship. And both of these men, along with other later prophets, desired to see the restoration of the true worship of God and of the Jerusalem Temple cultus in a better age (Jer. 31:6, 23; 33:18; Ezek. 40:1 to 48:35).

In speaking of the relationship of Yahweh to his people, the prophets often thought of the analogy of marriage. There are several instances in the prophetic writings, as well as elsewhere in the Old Testament, of the rather vivid use of this analogy. Chief among these is the description in Hos., chs. 1 to 3, of his own marriage to an unfaithful wife and of the way in which his experience exemplified that of Yahweh's with Israel. Although the actual circumstances of Hosea's unfortunate marriage relationship are not clear, the teaching that he derived from it is. Israel "commits great harlotry by forsaking the LORD" (ch. 1:2). She has gone after other lovers, the Baals (ch. 2:5–7), and she must be punished for her faithlessness (ch. 2:10–13). But the LORD will forgive her and restore her to himself in a renewed bond of love (ch. 2:14–23), just as Hosea had apparently brought back his own adulterous wife (ch. 3). The image of harlotry appears elsewhere in Hosea (e.g., chs. 4:10, 11–19; 5:3 f.; 6:10; 9:1), as well as in Isaiah (ch. 1:21), Jeremiah (ch. 2:20, 23 f.), and in a lurid and brutally frank allegory in Ezek., ch. 16 (cf. ch. 23).

Harlotry was but one way of describing Israel's idolatry and unfaithfulness to Yahweh. The prophets to a man condemned the worship of other gods in direct and unequivocal terms. Almost the entire book of Hosea is an elaboration of the theme of Israel's idolatry and the grief this has caused the LORD. Yet Hosea was sure that Yahweh would forgive and restore to himself his beloved people (chs. 2:14–23; 11:8; 14:1–7). Isaiah proclaimed judgment upon Judah's idolatry (ch. 2:6–11) and foresaw the coming destruction of all her idols (chs. 2:18–21; 17:7–11). Jeremiah spoke of Israel's apostasy at great length (ch. 2:1–37), and urged her to repent and to return to Yahweh (chs. 3:1 to 4:4). He also described Judah's degrading worship of idols with incense, wine, and oil, and even with human sacrifices (chs. 32:29 f.; 19:13; 7:16–20, 30–34). Ezekiel added further details regarding such abominations (ch. 8), plus a painfully clear vision of the glory of the LORD leaving his doomed Temple (chs. 10; 11:22–25). We know that during the eighth and seventh centuries foreign gods were repeatedly introduced into Israel and Judah.[14] There was ample reason for the prophets to become upset enough to say harsh things about the moral and religious corruption of their people. The people of the LORD had strayed far indeed from the ideal of what the LORD required of them!

GOD IN PAST, PRESENT, AND FUTURE

Involved as they were in the realities and exigencies of their own times, the Old Testament prophets did not lose sight of the meaning of contemporary events in the larger perspective of history. Their words were typically addressed to the immediate concerns of their own time, but, as we have seen before, they also projected God's present authority forward into future judgment and promise and backward into past events that impinged upon present situations. Thus it was essentially the present reality of God in history that most interested the prophets.[15]

During the period from Amos to Ezekiel there were numerous major events in the life of Israel that excited the imagination of the prophets in regard to Yahweh's role in history. The prophetic interpretation of the actual happenings of their time was always theocentric. They believed, as did the Deuteronomic historians, that Yahweh visited historical judgment upon his people in ways that should have made it clear to all that he was Lord of history. We often come across some form of the prophetic formula: "Thus says the Holy One of Israel, 'Because you despise this word, . . . therefore this iniquity shall be to you . . .'" (Isa. 30:12–13). Examples of the historical events that precipitated the prophets' proclamations of divine judgment, and redemption as well in many cases, may be briefly cited in support of these points.

The leading historical event of the eighth century in Northern Israel was of course the catastrophe that overtook that nation about 721 B.C., when the legions of Assyria destroyed Samaria and deported thousands of Israelites. One can see already in Amos and Hosea, shortly before the fall of Israel, the preview of Yahweh's punishment of that unhappy nation for her apostasy and immorality (Amos 2:6–8; 3:2; 5:1 to 6:14; Hos. 2:2–13; ch. 9), with some intimation that Assyria will be the instrument of Yahweh's judgment (e.g., Hos. 8:1). Isaiah, who lived in Jerusalem during the period of Israel's decline and demise, interpreted both the distress of Israel and the Assyrian threat to Judah as evidence of the effect of Yahweh's word of judgment (Isa. 9:8 to 10:4), but he also warned Assyria that Yahweh would bring her down in her great pride (chs. 10:5–19; 14:24–27; cf. Nahum, chs. 1 to 3). Micah similarly prophesied concerning the fall of Israel, both before (ch. 1:2–7) and after (ch. 2:12–13) the fact, assuming the LORD as the active agent in all these events.

In the seventh century the most significant development in Old Testament history was the successive subjugation of Judah by Assyria, Egypt, and Babylonia, the last-named empire finally crushing Judah and destroying Jerusalem about 586 B.C. The major prophets, Isaiah, Jeremiah, and Ezekiel, all had foreseen this eventuality, and Jeremiah and Ezekiel actually lived through it and spoke directly out of it (cf. also, Hab., chs. 1:1 to 2:5). Warnings to Judah that her iniquities would lead to her doom appear especially in Isaiah and Jeremiah (e.g., Isa. 1:1 to 5:24; 29:1–8; Jer. 4:5–31; 8:18 to 9:1; 12:7–13). But, again, these prophets also held that Yahweh would punish all wicked nations, including Assyria, Egypt, Babylonia,[16] and the smaller states surrounding Judah. The divine hand is now evident everywhere and in all of history. In Ezekiel, who began his prophetic ministry in the midst of Judah's devastation (ca. 593 B.C.), great blocks of material were given to his oracles concerning the fall of Judah (chs. 1 to 24) and to his hope for her eventual restoration (chs. 33 to 48). We shall come to such prophecies of restoration after considering briefly the prophets' understanding of the future "Day of the LORD."

Even before the final destruction of Israel and Judah her prophets had begun to look far ahead to a day when Yahweh would be acknowledged by all mankind as God and Lord, in the fullest possible meaning of these terms. At first their hope for such a day was undoubtedly grounded in a temporal and not too distant expectation—an expectation of better days upon the earth when wars would cease and men would dwell together in peace (e.g., Isa. 2:2–4; Micah 4:1–4). Much of what the prophets saw in the immediate future had to do with the restoration of the defeated and dispersed nations of Israel and Judah. Almost all the prophetic books contain some word of hope (Amos 9:11–15; Hos. 14:4–7; Isa. 4:2–6; 14:1 f.; Micah, chs. 4 and 5), and in Jeremiah and Ezekiel there are lengthy sections devoted to such promises of restoration (Jer., chs. 30 to 33; Ezek., chs. 37; 40 to 48). Gradually, however, these hopes seemed less and less a possibility for historical time, and the prophetic view of the future became more and more eschatological. At this point we must consider the idea of the Day of the LORD as a necessary prerequisite to the final days of blessing.

The prophets had come to believe that Yahweh's judgment must precede any possibility of redemption. The people were not returning to the LORD from their unfaithful ways, and, therefore, they would have to be tried and punished before they could be brought back into the right relationship with their God. The Day of the LORD was seen by the prophets as a time of punishment for Israel rather than for her enemies as the people thought (Amos 5:18–20; 8:9–14; Isa. 13:9–16; Zeph. 1:14–18). Many of the dire prophecies of doom in the prophetic literature begin with a reference to "that day," although it is often difficult to separate the eschatological passages from those with a more immediate temporal reference.[17]

The concepts of the Messiah and the Messianic Age also belong to the category of future expectations, and here, too, there is difficulty in deciding which specific passages are to be understood in an eschatological sense. Most of the prophecies that have to do with the Messiah (e.g., Isa. 9:2–7; 11:1–9; Micah 5:2–6) have been interpreted in futuristic terms by later commentators, but the idea of a Messiah clearly originated with the title (*mashiach*) given to the kings of Israel, beginning with Saul (see I Sam. 10:1). This title simply meant "Anointed One," and thus was applicable to all the historical monarchs, especially those of the lineage of David. This subject is much too complex to be discussed here, but there are numerous good treatises dealing with the Messiah idea and its ramifications.[18]

There is much more that could be said regarding the prophets' understanding of God's future purposes, and we shall return to this important theme in the next chapter. In this chapter we have attempted to stress the most important aspects or themes of the eighth- and seventh-century prophetic preaching, and we have tried to make clear in this last section particularly that for the prophets both the past and the future are of vital interest primarily as they have relevance for the present. Despite superficial impressions to the contrary, the prophets were men who more than anything else understood God in relation to the ultimate meaning of the here and now.

VII

God in the Later Prophetic View

THE UNKNOWN PROPHET

One of the most profound thinkers and gifted poets of the Old Testament was a prophet of the sixth century B.C. who is almost entirely unknown to us. We have at least a little information about most of the prophets—their lives, where they lived, their approximate dates, and in a few cases (Isaiah, Jeremiah) some biographical material relating their activities. But concerning our sixth-century prophet we know little beyond what his words tell us about his thought.

This unknown prophet is in one sense only a hypothetical character constructed out of the words and ideas recorded in Isa., chs. 40 to 55. These chapters are demonstrably different from the rest of The Book of Isaiah (chs. 1 to 39; 56 to 66). Chapters 1 to 39 are for the most part attributable to the eighth-century Isaiah of Jerusalem, about whom we have some historical information, and chs. 56 to 66 are sufficiently different to warrant attributing them to still another unknown author. As for chs. 40 to 55, this material first of all has a later historical context; it is set in the sixth century during Judah's exile and the rise of Persia under Cyrus the Great (see chs. 44:24 to 45:13) rather than in the eighth century. Secondly, its literary forms, style, and vocabulary are uniquely different from those of the First Isaiah, and of other Old Testament prophets for that matter. And, thirdly, the theological perspective of chs. 40 to 55 is one of hope, promise, comfort, and redemption for the exiled Judeans, whereas the First Isaiah spoke of God's coming judgment, punishment, and the destruction of his people and their nation. We must look upon The Book of Isaiah, therefore, as a three-part collection of prophetic oracles and other materials, the second part of which is a unit belonging to an anonymous author whom we may call Second Isaiah simply because his written words were at some point included in the literature attributed to Isaiah of Jerusalem.

The Second Isaiah (also called Deutero-Isaiah or Isaiah II) was probably born in Babylonia of exiled Jewish parents not long after the fall of Jerusalem and massive deportation of Judeans to Babylonia in 586 B.C. With genuine prophetic insight he saw in the rise of Cyrus of Persia, beginning about 546 B.C., the impending fulfillment of Yahweh's promised deliverance and restoration of his people. He felt that the time of Israel's necessary chastisement was drawing to a close, and that the future was bright with hope for those who would now be the redeemed of the LORD. Although we can say nothing with assurance concerning his life, there is much in his message that is worthy of our most careful attention. It is what this unusual servant of Yahweh had to say about God that most interests us. We shall see that he wrote with deep conviction and warm compassion on the hopeful idea of Israel's restoration. His denunciation and rejection of idolatry is as clear and forceful as that of any writer in the Old Testament. Moreover, he proclaimed in unmistakable terms the first statement of explicit monotheism in the Old Testament. There is no question that his understanding of God was monotheistic and universalistic in every respect. And perhaps his crowning achievement was the reinterpretation of Israel's role as that of God's "Suffering Servant," whose experience and example would be a light to the nations, to redeem and lead all mankind to the one true God.

So significant were the contributions of the unknown prophet that we shall want to devote most of this chapter to a discussion of his views of God and God's purposes, reserving only the last section of the chapter for a consideration of several of the post-exilic prophets.

WORDS OF COMFORT AND HOPE

The opening poetic words of Isa., chs. 40 to 55, sometimes called the "Book of Consolation," establish the tone and theme of the entire section:

> Comfort, comfort my people, says your God.
> Speak tenderly to Jerusalem, and cry to her
> that her warfare is ended,
>   that her iniquity is pardoned,
> that she has received from the LORD's hand
>   double for all her sins.
>
> (Ch. 40:1 f.)

The prophet believed that he had been summoned to proclaim the coming of the LORD to restore his people from exile, for they now had been redeemed from their iniquity. The culmination of Israel's historical and prophetical expectations resides in this proclamation and in the further promise that it holds forth.

In the preceding two centuries the prophets had been warning the LORD's people as forcefully as possible that their ways were leading directly to a time of judgment and punishment. When disaster came in the fall, first of Northern Israel, then of Judah, the interpretation of the prophets was obviously that this was the work of Yahweh. Since Israel's defeat and deportation effectively removed that nation from the stage of history, while the remnant of Judah was able to maintain itself and preserve its identity in Babylonian exile, the prophetic hope of restoration, both physical and spiritual, came to rest upon Judah, although Israel was never completely forgotten (see Isa. 11:11–16; 27:6; Jer. 30:4–8, 10 f.; 31:15–22). Thus the consoling words of the Second Isaiah are addressed to the condition of Judah in exile.[1]

The ground of such words of comfort and hope in Isa., ch. 40, is nothing other than the nature and purpose of Yahweh himself. It is not surprising that the poet moves directly from the initial consolation (ch. 40:1 f.) to the announcement of the LORD's coming (ch. 40:3–11), and thence to a paean in praise of God the Creator (ch. 40:12–20), the Lord of history (ch. 40:21–24), and the incomparable Holy One (ch. 40:25–31). Using this single chapter as a model, we may see in summary most of the leading ideas of Second Isaiah, or at the least, a sketch of his understanding of God's being and actions. Other chapters will of course add important concepts and descriptions to this summary (e.g., the Suffering Servant idea), but in ch. 40 we glimpse already something of the prophet's profound thought, earnest conviction, and beauty of expression.

One general caveat must be offered at this point. It is not really helpful or accurate to speak of the Second Isaiah's "view of God," as though it were somehow a complete and closed system, any more than it is correct to speak of "the Old Testament understanding of God" in this way. We have indicated before,[2] however, that in the use of these phrases we are quite conscious of the dynamic and developmental quality of Old Testament thought. What we want is to try to grasp something of the prophet's insight at the particular moment that he spoke or wrote, even though his views may have been somewhat different at other times. Many of the prophets, for example, expressed both despair and hope, warning and promise, judgment and deliverance. Although, in the case of Second Isaiah, the emphasis seems to be upon God's restoration of his people, his is definitely not a one-sided view of God and his purposes. That is to say, the words of comfort and hope are not sugarcoated "false" prophecies, like those spoken by the paid prophets of Jeremiah's day, but they are rooted in a profound awareness of God's continuing and active involvement in human history and of the consequences of this involvement, not only for Israel, but also for all the nations.

We shall discuss in a later section the degree to which this prophet thought that God's promise of the restoration of Israel would be actualized in history, as against its eschatological realization. In most of the Old Testament prophets there is a mixture of history and eschatology, to put it in a simplistic way, and the same is true of the Second Isaiah's message. He was well aware of Israel's past experience and of its meaning and place in the prophetic analysis of history. He was able to draw imaginatively upon the greatest events of the past (e.g., creation and the exodus) for the substance of his typologies of the present and the future. It was the future that seemed to interest him most—the immediate as well as the more remote future. Therefore, we cannot interpret the words of Second Isaiah, or of other Old Testament prophets for that matter, as though they belonged to only one dimension of time or history. At the same time, it is important to attempt to discover whether the prophet meant his words of assurance to be taken in a "literalistic" sense for the near future, or in a deeper sense as involving past, present, and future (here understood as *all* potential future times).

DENUNCIATION OF IDOLATRY

We have become aware already that the prophets of Israel had no tolerance whatsoever for idolatry. From Elijah's fanatic hatred of the Baal to Ezekiel's harsh descriptions of Jerusalem's harlotries, they unanimously agreed that idolatry had been the major reason for Israel's downfall, and that in every period of her history the people of Yahweh had been unfaithful to him. Second Isaiah added his voice to this prophetic clamor in a way that was, while not altogether new, certainly notable for its scornful tone and emphatic denial of the existence of other gods. Idols are nongods, was his theme, and it was this emphasis that largely helped to establish his general monotheistic argument.

The unknown prophet frequently set his denunciation of idolatry in juxtaposition with his assertion of the incomparable nature of God. To him, any attempt to compare the LORD God with idols was as ridiculous as comparing a living being with a dead tree.

> To whom then will you liken God,
>   or what likeness compare with him?
> The idol! a workman casts it,
>   and a goldsmith overlays it with gold,
>   and casts for it silver chains.
> He who is impoverished chooses for an offering
>   wood that will not rot;
> he seeks out a skilful craftsman
>   to set up an image that will not move.
>   (Isa. 40:18–20.)

The prophet wishes to make the point that the "gods" which people (including Israel) so vainly worship are *nothing* (nothing) more than the wood, metal, and stone materials shaped by the craftsman. In them there is no element of the genuinely sacred, the holy, the otherness of divinity. They are powerless to move, to act, to respond, or to save the people in any way (chs. 41:7, 23; 44:18–20; 45:20; 46:1 f., 5 f.; 48:5). Instead, in a time of distress and flight, it is the people who must save their gods!

One of the most devastating satires on idolatry to be found anywhere in religious literature is Second Isaiah's mocking account of the making of an idol (ch. 44:9–20). The reader should turn to this memorable passage and read it for himself, in the light of what has just been said about the folly of idolatry, in order to discover the full flavor of the prophet's ridicule. This prose passage was set in the midst of verses that recall Israel, God's servant, to her true relationship with her Creator (ch. 44:1–8, 21–22). The interpolation of the account of idol-making heightens the emphasis upon the uniqueness of the living God. The poor artisans who shape the iron and hew the wood so industriously are but men (v. 11), and the product of their craft is but a block of wood (v. 19). Yet the deluded mind of the workman (and of Israel) leads him to fall down and worship this man-made image, and to pray to it: "Deliver me, for thou art my god!" (v. 17). How blurred the vision of deity has become when man cannot distinguish a brute block of wood from the living God of Israel's history! Truly, "he feeds on ashes" (v. 20) who is unable to make this most crucial distinction.

To say that such idols are but inert images is to say also that the so-called gods of other nations, as we noted earlier, are not really gods at all (i.e., do not participate ontologically in the nature of deity). Assuming the mid-sixth-century date of the unknown prophet, and a roughly chronological arrangement of his oracles, we have in ch. 41:23 f. the first clearly explicit statement in the Old Testament denying the very existence of such "gods." The statement itself is not so important as the more general concept that it represents, but it is there, it is explicit, and it tells us that someone has finally put into concrete terms the monotheistic ideal that had been subconsciously or implicitly present in Israel's faith since the time of Moses, or more precisely, since the first prophets began to defend the claim of Yahweh's uniqueness against the claims of other gods.

Conceptually speaking, monotheism requires on the negative side just such a rejection of the possible existence of other gods, as well as the positive assertion that Yahweh (or some other deity) alone is God. Second Isaiah posited both aspects of the concept, grounded as always in the Old Testament more upon an awareness of Israel's empirical past than upon a speculative abstraction, and thus he became the first truly monotheistic thinker in the Old Testament.

MONOTHEISM AND HISTORY IN SECOND ISAIAH

Let us look further into the monotheism of the Second Isaiah. Having observed that the prophet frequently related his attacks upon idol worship to the incomparability of God, we may now ask what it is that puts God out of the range of comparison with the idols of man. Did Second Isaiah arrive at some new insights concerning the nature of God, or was his understanding merely the culmination of centuries of Israelite faith?

In Isa., ch. 40, God is depicted as creator of the universe, an idea that may go back beyond the time of Moses. The prophet's cosmogonic terminology and imagery are similar to the forms of expression employed in certain psalms (Ps. 33:13 f.; 104), and in the Wisdom Literature (e.g., Prov. 8:22–31; Job 22:14; 38:4–38), and in general his tripartite cosmology (heavens, earth, waters) parallels that of Gen., ch. 1. But the point of Second Isaiah's extolling God as "Creator of the ends of the earth" (ch. 40:28) is that this claim cannot be made for the idols constructed by man. Only the LORD, the everlasting God, has created the universe, and there is none to whom he may be likened (ch. 40:18, 25). It seems almost that the writer is arguing from the fact of God's creation of all things to the assertion of his uniqueness. In one verse he moves from his description of the LORD, "who created the heavens . . .

who formed the earth and made it," to Yahweh's own statement:
"I am the LORD, and there is no other" (ch. 45:18).

It is probably more correct, however, to say that Second Isaiah's
monotheistic understanding either preceded or was confluent with
his ideas of God as Creator, Redeemer, Lord of history, and so on.
He was primarily concerned to uphold Yahweh's uniqueness
against the claims made for other "gods." In this respect he declared repeatedly that the idols were not gods and that there were
no other gods besides the LORD (chs. 41:24, 28 f.; 42:8; 43:10, 13;
44:6, 8; 45:5–6, 14, 18; 46:9). His emphasis upon Yahweh as
Creator of all was simply consistent with his universalistic understanding of Yahweh as the one God of all.

Second Isaiah's monotheism is further apparent in those passages which speak of God as Redeemer of his people and of all
mankind (through Israel as the Servant), as King, as Covenant
Maker, and as Lord of history. The concept of Yahweh as universal Redeemer, exemplified in the imagery of the Servant, is one
of Second Isaiah's most important contributions to religious
thought, and we shall consider it more fully in the following
section. God's kingship is mainly a corollary to his Lordship over
history, which is a basic assumption in all the prophetic writings.
In one rather long passage (chs. 51:17 to 52:12), the announcement to Zion, "Your God reigns," comes as the climax to a description of the LORD's punishment and eventual restoration of
Jerusalem (cf. ch. 43:14 f.). The central concern of the entire
section is clearly to celebrate the LORD's rule over the events of
history. It is in this context also that we are to understand the
reference to the covenant in various passages in Isa., chs. 40 to 55.

In regard to the immediate history in which the unknown
prophet found himself, we have mentioned already that he must
have witnessed the decline of Babylonia and the rise of Persia as
the major power in the eastern Mediterranean or Near Eastern
world. Cyrus, King of Persia, conquered Babylonia in 539 B.C. and
was soon master of a vast empire reaching from Asia Minor and
Egypt in the west almost to India in the east. Second Isaiah saw in
these events, and in Cyrus' release of the exiled Jews, the hand of
Yahweh, whose historical purpose had begun with creation and

was now moving on to its *telos* or final end in redemption. In this total plan Cyrus played a significant part. He was Yahweh's agent who began the redemptive phase of divine history by his victories over the nations (chs. 41:1 to 42:4). Cyrus, although not aware of his role as God's agent (ch. 45:5), could be called "my shepherd" (ch. 44:28) and the "anointed" (Messiah) of the Lord (ch. 45:1). This somewhat startling thought, that Yahweh could so look upon and designate an alien king as Israel's savior, is not at all inconsistent with the prophetic view of history. Other nations had been considered to be instruments of the Lord's wrath by previous prophets, and Second Isaiah merely made this concept more specific. He did not go on to specify the exact manner of Cyrus' redemptive work, however; the oracles in chs. 44:24 to 45:13 are more rhetorical than factual. We learn from other sources (Ezra 1:1-4; the Cyrus Cylinder) that Cyrus did release the Jews from exile in Babylonia, and that some of them did return to Jerusalem to attempt to restore their nation. The unknown prophet's view of God's purposes in history then moves beyond these present events to a future time that will transcend history in its greater redemptive significance.

God as Redeemer and Re-Creator

In the Old Testament a variety of Hebrew verbs are used to describe God's redemptive activities. He "delivers," "saves," "gathers," "restores," "ransoms," or "redeems" his people, depending upon the individual speaker and the situation to which he has reference. Second Isaiah uses several of these verbs in his promises to exiled Israel, but his preference actually is for the noun form "Redeemer" as a title for the Lord. The etymology of this word is rather complex, and for our purposes it is sufficient to observe that it can denote variously "vengeance," "vindication," "ransom," or "release." In the usage of Second Isaiah, God acts as Redeemer first of all through his restoration of Israel from exile to her own land—an act that lends the idea of Savior also to the title Redeemer. Regardless of the specific denotation of the term, it is clear that the prophet wishes to express throughout the idea that it is Yahweh alone, the Holy One of Israel, who will act on behalf of his chosen ones to do what he purposes for them.

Second Isaiah saw Israel's release from exile and return to Jerusalem as a kind of new exodus. Using the typology of the exodus from Egypt, he thought of Israel's bondage in a foreign country, her deliverance by a mighty act of God, her journey through the wilderness, and her return to the Promised Land in terms of the parallels between that earlier experience and the events of his own time. The LORD will break the bars of his people's imprisonment and turn their captor's shouting into lamentation (chs. 43:14; 48:20; 49:9, 24–26). He will divide the waters so that his people may pass through (ch. 43:16 f.), as he did at the Red Sea, and will lead them by a smooth path and provide for them in the wilderness (chs. 41:17–20; 42:16 f.; 43:19; 48:21; 49:9–11). And Zion, the holy place of the LORD, will once more be inhabited and blessed (ch. 49:14–21). The same themes are also treated in a long intercessory poem in Third Isaiah (chs. 63:7 to 64:12), where the spirit is one of petition rather than of promise.

In Second Isaiah's typological use of the exodus and creation stories the emphasis is upon renewal as well as upon redemption. One can almost say that the prophet is looking forward to a new creation and a new return (to Jerusalem and to the LORD) in a sense that is transhistorical. For this reason, it is tempting to speculate upon the relationship of his concept of renewal to the classic myth of the eternal return, found in many ancient religions,[3] but this would lead us too far afield in a survey of this kind. In any case, we can be sure that the unknown prophet never lost sight of the significance of actual historical events in his interpretation of God's plans, as he saw in Cyrus a concrete example of God's immediate redemptive activity.

The most dramatic redemptive figure in Second Isaiah is that of the Suffering Servant.[4] There has been some speculation that the poems in which this figure is central were not composed by the person who wrote the rest of Isa., chs. 40 to 55, but the evidence for such a theory is not really convincing. The Servant poems fit in quite well with everything we have already seen in Second

Isaiah's thinking and writing. He believes in one God, who is Creator of the universe, and who will redeem his people. A natural extension of such basic beliefs is that God will redeem all creation, all of mankind. What is new and unusual in the Servant imagery is that Israel will serve in a special capacity as the agent of the divine plan of redemption. Although there is some ambiguity on the point, it is the view of most Old Testament scholars that Israel is indeed the Servant in these passages. This fact is specifically stated in a few cases (ch. 49:3; cf. chs. 41:8; 44:1–2; 45:4). Some references seem to have an individual in mind as the Servant (chs. 42:1–4; 49:6; 50:4–6), perhaps someone like Jeremiah (chs. 49:1, 5; 53:7 f.; cf. Jer. 1:5; 11:18 f.), or even the prophet himself (Isa. 50:4–6). It is also possible that the writer had both the nation and an individual in mind, but it is more likely that he simply personified the nation, as was so often done by Old Testament writers, and thus spoke of Israel in the singular.[5]

The Servant was chosen by the LORD to bring justice to the nations (ch. 42:1–4), to restore the LORD's people (ch. 49:5 f.), and to serve God even when shamefully mistreated (ch. 50:4–11). In the fourth Servant poem (chs. 52:13 to 53:12) the theme of the Servant's rejection and suffering is eloquently elaborated. Even though the Servant (Israel) has been brutally disfigured (chs. 52:14; 53:2 f.), God will exalt him before the nations (ch. 52:13, 15). Men have despised him and rejected him, but by his vicarious suffering, bearing "the iniquity of us all," he was able to restore all men to God (ch. 53:4–6). The Servant was completely subject to the will of the LORD, and God's judgment and mercy were manifested through his experience (vs. 10–12). The mission of the Servant is perhaps most concisely stated in these lines:

> I will give you as a light to the nations,
> that my salvation may reach to the end of the earth.
> (Ch. 49:6.)

The prophet must have had in mind Israel's experience during the Babylonian exile when he spoke of the Servant's suffering. He was able to see in her physical and spiritual disasters the plan of God for Israel and for all people. He interpreted Israel's unfortunate personal tragedy in a radically positive way, not merely as deserved punishment, but as an experience that offered vicarious atonement for all who would see in it the presence of God. And this possibility was open to *all* nations. This, then, is the universalism of Second Isaiah which is such an important corollary to his whole monotheistic point of view.

Was Second Isaiah thinking in eschatological terms when he wrote about God as Redeemer? In some respects it would seem so, especially when he envisions the glorious conditions of the future (e.g., chs. 40:3–5, 9–11; 44:1–5; 49:7–13; ch. 55). But much of what we see pictured in such expressions of future hope must be received as the spontaneous and poetic utterances of a joyous prophetic spirit. There is much of poetic imagery, simile, and hyperbole, but little of the technical terminology of eschatology. Moreover, there is an urgency and immediacy in the prophet's message that convinces us of his assurance of God's activity on behalf of his people without delay. We have no impression of a kind of disappointed postponement of the new creation and the redeemed community to an indefinite future age. Yet, at the same time, in all of this there is a sense of transcendence, of events moving in a dimension beyond human history and time. The prophet is not bound by merely temporal categories, and he understands that the ways of God are not the ways of men. We may conclude, therefore, that while he concentrated upon the promise of the near future for Israel and for all mankind, he was not unaware of the purposes of God for a more radical transformation in a time beyond this present age.

The influence of Second Isaiah's ideas, notably that of the Servant, on later Christian thought is worthy of particular notice. Although some commentators have seen in the Servant a Messianic figure, the concept of one who humbly and meekly suffers shame and abuse for the sake of others is hardly Messianic in any traditional sense. Early Christianity saw the fulfillment of certain Messianic expectations in Jesus, but it was also able to identify his experience with that of the Suffering Servant to a remarkable degree. The doctrine of sacrificial atonement goes back ultimately to the sacrificial practice of ancient Israel, but Christian interpretation owes much to the picture drawn by Second Isaiah. And for that matter, later religious thought, both Christian and Jewish, received a tremendous contribution from the unknown prophet, whose message of comfort and hope, denial of the existence of other gods, explicit and highly developed monotheism, and interpretation of Yahweh in history as Creator and Redeemer greatly illuminate our whole understanding of God.

THE POSTEXILIC PROPHETS

We face a difficult problem in trying to describe the understanding of God that is present in the several postexilic prophetic books. In the first place, they represent a considerable variety of literary genres, from the narrative styles of Haggai, Zechariah, and Jonah to the apocalyptic poetry of Joel and Daniel. In the second place, the theological perspectives of Jews in the postexilic or Persian period (ca. 539–331 B.C.) were more diversified than at perhaps any other time in Jewish history, due in large measure to the many external influences on Judaism[6] during this period. And, in the third place, none of these prophetic writers concentrated upon a *theology* as such, i.e., upon a systematic expression of their concept of God. But, for that matter, neither did the other writers of Old Testament books whose ideas we have been discussing, so that the problem is not new to us. In view of these factors, our best procedure will be to look briefly at the most important ideas of each of the postexilic prophets as they help in our understanding of the God of the Old Testament.

The prophets Haggai and Zechariah must be considered together, since they were contemporaries who were concerned about the same problems in the restored Jerusalem community about 520 B.C. Strangely enough, their major concerns were to see the Temple at Jerusalem rebuilt and the ritual worship resumed. These are not at all typical of the prophetic interests we have previously encountered, quite apart from the specific historical context of these two prophets, but we find here the beginning of a transition to a more cultic orientation of the later prophets.[7] Haggai believed that the LORD desired such cultic projects to be completed before anything else (Hag. 1:2–4, 7–11), and that following this, the LORD would establish the Kingdom and would designate Zerubbabel, the governor of Jerusalem, as the Messiah (Hag. 2:20–23). In a series of apocalyptic visions Zechariah[8] expressed his convictions that the LORD willed the restoration of Jerusalem and the Temple (Zech. 1:16 f.), that the exiles should return to the LORD (Zech. 2:6–13), and that the Messianic Age was about to begin (Zech. 6:1–8). Like Haggai, this prophet believed that the Messianic figure, the Branch, was someone already present and waiting to be acknowledged—either Zerubbabel (Hag. 2:20–23) or Joshua (Zech. 3:8; 6:11 f.). Using the title "LORD of hosts" repeatedly (see Zech., ch. 8), Zechariah also described in some detail how even the nations would come to seek the LORD in Jerusalem. Both Haggai and Zechariah represent a kind of prophecy that moves rather awkwardly from mundane matters, if the affairs of temple and cultus can be so designated, to somewhat esoteric and grandiose hopes, without adding greatly to our knowledge of the nature and will of the Old Testament God.

In The Book of Malachi (ca. 500–450 B.C.) we have a prophetic message (Malachi = "My messenger") that is almost entirely involved with priestly concerns. The prophet, about whom nothing is said in the book, spoke in quite prosaic manner about the necessity for faithful worship as a means of honoring the covenant with God (chs. 2:4 f., 10–12; 4:4). He condemned the corrupt worship practices of the Temple priests—the sacrifice of unacceptable animals, for example (ch. 1:6–8, 13 f.)—and their false teaching of the people (ch. 2:7–9). He believed that God was distressed by such things, and also by divorce (vs. 10–16), injustice (ch. 3:5), and failure to give the tithes (vs. 8 f.). But God will bless the faithful (vs. 10–12), and when the Day of the LORD comes (chs. 3:2; 4:1, 5) there will be judgment upon evildoers (chs. 3:5; 4:1), while those who feared the LORD will be recorded in "a book of remembrance" (ch. 3:16). The writer's description of the "messenger" who would proclaim the LORD's coming (chs. 3:1–4; 4:5 f.) is of considerable interest for later New Testament concepts (cf. Matt. 11:10; Mark 1:2; Luke 1:17;

7:27). This prophet was also among the few Old Testament thinkers to speak of the fatherhood of God (Mal. 2:10) and its implications for mankind.

Joel is another little-known prophetic figure, who seems to have lived in Judah late in the Persian period, perhaps 400 to 350 B.C. His book has so many liturgical and priestly overtones that it must have come out of a cultic context. Yet its central theme is purely prophetic in the traditional sense. He saw in a devastating locust plague a warning of God's impending judgment on the Day of the LORD (Joel 1:1 to 2:27). The coming of God's judgment will be marked by a universal outpouring of the spirit (ch. 2:28 f.) and by unusual signs and portents (ch. 2:30–32). God's universality is severely restricted, however, for deliverance and restoration are for Judah and Jerusalem (ch. 3:1–3, 20 f.; cf. ch. 2:32), whereas "the nations" will be judged and punished (ch. 3:1–21). There are echoes of the eighth-century prophets everywhere in Joel, curiously modified by his emphasis upon cultic features (see chs. 1:13 f.; 2:1, 12–16; 3:17). In Joel, God seems once more to be understood in most respects just as the preexilic prophets knew him.

We encounter a view greatly different, however, in The Book of Jonah. Again, we know little historically of this obscure prophet, although a few references place him in the first half of the eighth century B.C. The Book of Jonah was not produced at that time, but from the evidence within the material itself it must have been written in the fourth or third century B.C. The book is most unprophetic in that it contains a didactic story rather than a series of poetic oracles. Moreover, the narrative itself is not so important as the main theme that it so artfully proclaims. The author of Jonah had only one message—that God's love, mercy, and forgiveness are extended in a truly universal way to all people. The dramatic narrative of the reluctant Jewish prophet who is finally forced to preach this saving message merely serves as an effective vehicle for the writer's basic belief. God is one, he is the God of all nations, and his salvation is offered universally. With this conviction the author of Jonah joins the Second Isaiah among the most liberal and progressive "theologians" of the Old Testament.

Finally, The Book of Daniel, much later than any other prophetic book,[9] a product of the late Greek period of Jewish history probably to be dated 167–164 B.C., offers a thoroughly apocalyptic view of God's reality in past, present, and future events. When we ask what contribution the remarkable stories and visions that constitute this book make to the Old Testament understanding of God, we face the problem of the whole style of thinking and writing called apocalyptic. An apocalypse is simply a revelation, but the term now refers technically to revelations in times of distress and persecution that symbolically relate past events to present experiences and to hopes of a triumphant and peaceful future. Such visions are thoroughly theocentric, coming out of a time when men must put their complete trust in God since everything around them has failed or is being destroyed.

In Daniel this trust is expressed largely in terms of obeying the Jewish laws within the covenant relationship. The author of Daniel was either a priest or someone whose theological perspective was determined by a feeling for the ultimate importance of legalistic religious obligations. He emphasized such requirements as the dietary laws (Dan., ch. 1), worship of no other gods or idols (ch. 3), and upholding the sanctity of holy vessels (ch. 5), but in fairness we must also note the author's deep concern for recognition of God's wisdom (ch. 2), his power (ch. 4), and his protection of those who faithfully serve him (ch. 6). The familiar stories that convey these thoughts were written to encourage Jews to remain faithful to their God during the days of terrible persecution under the Seleucid (Greek) ruler Antiochus IV Epiphanes (167–164 B.C.). In addition, Daniel contains four dream-visions that portray the eventual victory of the people of God over their enemies. The apocalyptic language and imagery of these visions actually heightens rather than obscures the concept of God as ruler of all things who will bring about that glorious *eschaton* that his faithful people always believed in. Thus, we may say that the prophetic understanding of God in the Old Testament never lost sight of God's sole sovereignty, and in Daniel this understanding reached a fitting conclusion on a note of optimistic and triumphant faith.

VIII

God and the Religion of Israel

The Nature of Israelite Religion

In this chapter we shall examine the religion of Israel as a system or pattern of integrated concepts working together in the attempt to actualize a relationship with God. It is the concern to establish and continue such a relationship that makes religion vital. To be *involved* with deity must be the principal motivation and quality of anything that we would call "religious."

We can say that "religion" usually refers to the more formal, institutional, and even external aspects of this involvement with deity or God. As such, it includes places, objects, actions, persons, and times that are considered to be sacred, as we shall see below. Religion, in this sense, refers particularly to the devotional life of a group or a nation. But there must be concepts and beliefs underlying the several aspects of the sacred, and we need to learn first what were some of these concepts and beliefs in Israelite religion. We have, of course, discussed a number of these ideas in preceding chapters, but here we shall look at a few additional concepts having to do especially with the worship of God in the Old Testament.

It is important to deal with this subject in a concise and especially in a descriptive manner, as we have attempted to do throughout this survey. We are not interested here in evaluating the Old Testament ideas of God and religion from a particular perspective, but in describing, explaining, and understanding them. As we talk about religious ideas, beliefs, and practices in ancient Israel, no value judgments will be offered. Each religion of mankind is "true" to the believer who accepts it, and all other tests of religious truth are relative. The religion of Israel, therefore, is a phenomenon in history, the major expression of which is contained in the Old Testament writings, and what we have to say about it here must accurately reflect the meaning of those writings.

Of the many features that characterize the religion of Israel, perhaps the most outstanding is an emphasis upon obedience to the law of God. This feature pertains to the formal, as well as to the internal, aspects of the religion. In the Ten Commandments, for example, we find three requirements that are essential to Israel's devotional life. The First Commandment, "You shall have no other gods before me," asserts that for Israel no other gods may be worshiped, a requirement that explicitly distinguished her religion from the polytheistic cults of her time. In the Second Commandment, "You shall not make for yourself a graven image," the worship of Yahweh is further separated from the ancient world's worship of the images and idols of personified natural forces. The reason given for this prohibition is instructive: Yahweh is "a jealous God," who is "showing steadfast love" (covenant faithfulness) to those who love and obey him. And in the Fourth Commandment, "Remember the sabbath day, to keep it holy," we find the fundamental sacred time, to be set apart from other times as a day of rest and as a commemoration of the LORD's day of rest following the Creation. Thus we have here the paradigm of both the Sabbath of Judaism and the Lord's Day of Christianity.

These commandments indicate only part of the basic nature of Israelite religion, for the requirements that give form to this religion practically fill the books of Exodus, Leviticus, Numbers, and Deuteronomy. Many of these laws, however, relate to conduct apart from worship, which is our immediate concern here, and so they do not inform us regarding Israel's piety. In such diverse documents as Genesis, Judges, Samuel, Kings, Psalms, Ezra, and Nehemiah we may learn more about the practice of religion in Israel's history. And in all of this we shall want to discover what the religion of Israel tells us about her understanding of God.

One additional aspect of Israelite religion must be noted at this point, and that is that many of the Old Testament sources are colored by a Priestly point of view. This is due to the fact that Jewish priests during the Babylonian exile and for some time thereafter were responsible for the collecting and final editing of many books in the Hebrew Bible, notably those of the Pentateuch and Psalms. This fact suggests at least that Priestly interests, for example, in the Torah (Law), the Temple, and religious ritual, took their place alongside those of historians, prophets, sages, and others. And, in many cases, we must be aware of a close interrelationship among some of these groups, for they clearly were not isolated from one another. In this connection, the joint efforts of priests and prophets in the worship of God will be discussed later in this chapter. And we shall also have more to say about the contribution of the Priestly perspective to the religion of Israel.

GOD AS THE HOLY ONE

The requirement of obedience to divine law assumes an authority who demands and is worthy of such obedience. For Israel, Yahweh was just such an authority. Beyond the ideas of Yahweh as Creator, Covenant Maker, King, Righteous One, Lord of history, and so on, was there something more that commanded Israel's response in worship and service, in short, in religion? The answer to this question is best given in the understanding of God as the Holy One of Israel.

Behind the Old Testament concept of God's holiness lies the primitive idea of fearful demonic power. The idea of holiness[1] originally had to do with the numinous quality of whatever was thought to be separate from or beyond the ordinary and human aspects of existence. Rudolf Otto called this quality in its awesome dimension the *mysterium tremendum,* and he applied the term "Wholly Other" to the nature of that which we call God.

In the Old Testament there are numerous references to the feeling of awesomeness or fear in response to the LORD's "terrible," "dreadful," or "fearful" nature (e.g., Gen. 15:12; 28:17; Ex. 19:24; 20:18–20; Deut. 7:21; 10:17). "The fear of the LORD" is an expression regularly used for reverence or piety in the Old Testament (Gen. 20:11; II Sam. 23:3; II Chron. 19:9; Job 28:28; Ps. 19:9; 111:10; many times in Proverbs), and to "fear" the LORD may mean to worship him. The dread or terror felt by primitive people confronted by some phenomenon totally outside their range of experience and understanding is thus preserved in the Hebrew idea of God's holiness.

In addition to the numinous quality of deity expressed by the terms just mentioned, the holiness of God includes his separateness from all things earthly or profane. He is Wholly Other in the sense that nothing on earth is like him or participates in his nature. He is holy or sacred just because he is other than what we are or anything else is. The Old Testament makes a sharp distinction between what is sacred and what is profane, but it is not unaware of the relationship between the two. There is access to the sacred. The holiness of Yahweh prevented the Israelites from ascending his sacred mountain, but Moses and Aaron could approach the LORD by his permission (Ex. 19:10–24). The prophet Isaiah encountered the terrible presence of the LORD in the Jerusalem Temple and feared for his life, but was cleansed and given a divine commission to be the LORD's spokesman (Isa., ch. 6). The transference of the quality of holiness from God to something ordinarily considered profane will be discussed below in the section on the sacred.

The holiness of God also came to include the idea of his righteousness. At first, there was no intrinsic ethical content in the understanding of God as the Holy One. As we have seen, his holiness was conceived as dread majesty and otherness. The Hebrew word for "holy" could even be used of the sacred prostitutes of Canaanite religion, who were consecrated or set apart in their service to the god Baal, and the use of the word here obviously lacks positive ethical meaning. In the case of Yahweh, holiness meant separation, and this included separation from the profane and unclean, and thus from everything evil or sinful. From this it follows that Yahweh is completely good, morally righteous, and from this his holiness came to mean also his righteousness (see above, pp. 99–101). The older idea of God's awesomeness is not forgotten, however, and in passages such as Isa. 6:1–13 we find the primitive and the ethical ideas closely intermingled. The Holiness Code in Lev., chs. 17 to 26, to which we shall return, also reflects this intermingling at a time probably later even than that of Isaiah.

The idea of God as the Holy One obviously has many implications for the religion of Israel. It is basic to the response of reverence and worship that we are considering in this chapter. Israel responded to Yahweh because he was historically her covenant God, her protector, benefactor, and Lord. But the ability of God to command such obedience and respect lay in his awesome, majestic power. There can be no doubt that Israel actually "feared" the LORD in the sense of terror and dread. But as Israel came to know this awesome Being in history, she also learned to "fear" him in reverence and worship. The idea of reverence never completely lost the primitive sense of fear, but it was channeled into manifold forms of religious devotion and thus became a significant element in Israel's worship of God.

GOD'S HOLINESS AND MAN'S HOLINESS

"And the LORD said to Moses, 'Say to all the congregation of the people of Israel, You shall be holy; for I the LORD your God am holy.'" (Lev. 19:1 f.; cf. 20:26.) With this statement the Holiness Code in Lev., chs. 17 to 26, sums up the responsibility of man's holiness in response to God's holiness. The LORD's command in this case does not mean that the people are somehow to participate in the numinous quality of God's holiness. The distinction between man and God in this regard is never blurred in the Old Testament. The LORD's command means in essence that Israel is to be holy as the special, separated people of the holy God. Their holiness is derived from him and is maintained by their faithfulness to him and to his will. In Leviticus the repeated phrase, "I am the LORD your God," serves to remind Israel of the sole source of her own sacredness.

The commandments in the Holiness Code have to do both with ritual and ethical requirements. They are designed to keep the people pure and separated from that which is profane and unclean. From the Priestly perspective, which left its indelible imprint upon these laws, man's holiness was constituted by his obedience to God in all things, and specifically in those ways prescribed in the codes of conduct for cultic life, or worship, and for moral life. This was "religion" to the priests, and it was in such codes that they attempted to embody their understanding of covenant-keeping and of the standards of behavior implicit in the covenant requirements.

To sin is to violate any of God's requirements in any way. This is sin[2] first of all because it is fundamentally self-assertion against God's will, as in the disobedience of Adam and Eve (Gen., ch. 3; cf. 4:7). It is sin also because it breaks the bond of relationship between man and God provided for essentially in the covenant. And it is sin because the violater loses the holiness derived from his closeness to God, and thus becomes a completely profane person.

As a ritual requirement, holiness is actually a state of being. A man does not possess holiness as a part of his nature or as an immutable quality. He is holy when he participates in God's holiness, and he is unholy when he breaks away from God's requirements into the profane sphere. Man's holiness, therefore, is a total responsibility for his whole being and for everything in his life. It is especially related to his worship of God, for it is in worship that he comes closest to a realization of the sacred potential in his life and in all of existence. According to the Old Testament, God has made it possible for man to approach him, as it were, through actions that involve him in the sacred, indeed, that are themselves a part of what is holy or sacred.

The worship of God in ancient Israel is important to us in this survey because it opens another dimension of the Old Testament understanding of God. The whole of Israel's worship, which is in a real sense the very substance of her *religion*, cannot be discussed here. We are attempting to delineate and to define the most characteristic and significant aspects of Israel's religion in order to discover what religion, as defined earlier, can tell us about God. To this point we have seen that obedience to God as the Holy One (originally as the Fearful or Awesome One) is a basic feature in Israel's religion, and that man's holiness is derived solely from his faithful response to God, especially in worship. The concept of God's holiness involves the view that those things are holy or sacred which are maintained within the boundaries of his requirements, i.e., in closeness to the Holy One. We may now turn to a consideration of those features in the religion of Israel that were thought to participate in sacredness, after which we shall have more to say on the subject of Israel's worship of God.

GOD AND THE SACRED

Having already discussed the meaning of God's holiness and the nature of the sacred as it relates to man, we must here look briefly at more specific aspects of the sacred as manifested in Israel's religion. These aspects can best be treated under the following headings:

1. *Sacred places.* From earliest times there was the recognition among the Hebrews that certain places were sacred. They were obviously made sacred by something very special associated with them, most often a theophany or appearance of God at the place. Genesis records a number of such places. At Shechem near "the oak of Moreh" Abraham built an altar and worshiped the LORD (Gen. 12:6 f., J tradition), as he did also by "the oaks of Mamre" at Hebron (Gen. 13:18; 18:1). God found the fleeing Hagar at a sacred well called Beer-la-hai-roi, "Well of One Who Sees and Lives" (Gen. 16:7, 13 f.), and later provided water for Hagar and Ishmael near Beer-sheba (Gen. 21:14, 17–20). Isaac also encountered God at Beer-sheba, and worshiped him at an altar he built there (Gen. 26:23–25). Because of a dream in which God appeared to him, Jacob named the place where he had slept Bethel, "House of God" (Gen. 28:10–22), and it later became the location of a major sanctuary in the Northern Kingdom. In

another night experience, Jacob wrestled with "a man," apparently representing God, and named the place where this event occurred Peniel, "face of God" (Gen. 32:22–30).

There are numerous examples of this kind of thing, where the appearance of the Deity sanctifies a place, which is then named accordingly. Other places came to be sacred in similar ways. Perhaps the best known of these was Mt. Sinai (or Horeb), where Yahweh first appeared to Moses (Ex. 3:1 to 4:17) and where Israelite tradition places the great theophany that resulted in the giving of the Law (Ex. 19:1–24). We note that God could appear anywhere, but that certain places were more sacred to him. During the period when Israel wandered in the wilderness, God accompanied them and dwelt in the sacred Tabernacle.[3] As the Israelites moved into Canaan they found again the old sacred places at Beer-sheba, Shechem, Hebron, and Bethel, and added to these the names of Shiloh, Dan, and Jerusalem. The last named is outstanding in importance because it was the location of Israel's most holy place, the Temple.

The Judean "Deuteronomic" traditions in the Old Testament attempted to make the Jerusalem Temple the *only* sacred place for Israel. The law of the central sanctuary in Deut. 12:1–31 specified that all local shrines were to be abandoned, even destroyed, and that the people must worship only in "the place which the LORD your God will choose." This law apparently provided the authority for the extensive reform effected by King Josiah in the late seventh century B.C. (see II Kings, chs. 22; 23). Jerusalem had been chosen by David as his capitol, the Temple was then built by Solomon on a site where David had placed an altar to the LORD (II Sam. 24:18–25; I Chron. 22:1; II Chron. 3:1), and the city has from those days been sacred to Jews, as well as later to Christians and Muslims.

2. *Sacred objects.* We may mention briefly some examples of sacred objects that are often associated with sacred places. The altars built at various sacred places were themselves thought to be holy, as were also the trees, wells, pillars, and other objects associated with such places.[4] These objects could include almost anything, natural or man-made, that might represent some aspect

of sacredness. They were sacred not only because of an event with which they might have been associated, but also because of sacred actions, such as sacrifice, prayer, and the like, repeated where the objects were and often employing them in the action, or because of their use by sacred persons.

The ritual laws of Exodus and Leviticus refer to a large number of sacred objects. The most important of these was undoubtedly the Ark of the Covenant, a chest or box that contained various holy things, such as the Tables of the Law and possibly a jar of manna and Aaron's rod (Ex. 25:16, 21; 16:33 f.; Num. 17:10). Its greatest significance, however, was that it represented the presence of God himself (Ex. 25:10–22), and was such a powerful symbol that it was considered a taboo object (see II Sam. 6:1–11).[5] We have already shown (in Ch. III) the immense importance of the Ark as a symbol of Yahweh leading his hosts into battle, and during the days of the Jerusalem Temple the Ark occupied the Holy of Holies, the most sacred place in the innermost part of the sanctuary.

Other sacred objects listed in the ritual laws include altars, lamps, utensils of many kinds, and hangings for Tabernacle and Temple. Also considered to be sacred were all the things pertaining to the priests, such as their garments, including the ephod (Ex. 28:6–12), the sacred lots (Urim and Thummim, Ex. 28:30), and whatever was offered or sacrificed. The last named had to be ritually clean or sacred, according to the detailed specifications of Lev., ch. 11 (cf. ch. 20:22–26).

We must keep in mind that these objects did not possess intrinsic holiness in Israelite religious thought, for such an idea could lead to idolatry, as the prophetic writers were so well aware. Rather, the holy things were those things consecrated or set apart for the LORD, dedicated to his holy name and thus separated from all that was profane. And this understanding could apply equally to anything from certain portions of the sacrifice (e.g., Lev. 22:1) to the entire complex of the Temple.

3. *Sacred actions.* All acts of worship are considered sacred because they involve the recognition and the invocation of the Holy One, and because they are usually performed in sacred

places and in association with sacred objects, persons, and times. What the worshiper does may symbolize, dramatize, and even actualize his relationship with God and his perception of the sacred in his own religious experience.

The Old Testament recognizes hardly any other sacred action as having the importance of offering or sacrifice. It is true that prayer must be considered a meaningful sacred action, and there are many examples of prayers being offered to God. A verbal petition to God, however, was usually considered a community enterprise to be performed by the priests rather than by individuals. Instances of individuals praying to the LORD are most often cast in the form of a conversation, especially in the older narratives, but in Psalms we do have numerous prayers of individuals, as well as those of the community or nation. The psalms indicate also that in the liturgy of later times pilgrimages to the Temple, singing or chanting, and the general observance of special festivals were included in worship. Indeed, the book of Psalms has often been called the "Hymnbook of the Second Temple."[6]

The subject of offerings and sacrifices is much too vast to be treated adequately here. It will be sufficient to make a few general observations in line with the main theme of this chapter. We know that primitive Hebrew religion must have looked upon sacrifice as normative to a recognition of the Deity. The early literature of Genesis has preserved stories of animal sacrifices in the legends of the ancestors (e.g., Abel in Gen. 4:4; Noah in ch. 8:20) and in the stories of the patriarchs (Abraham in chs. 15:9–11, 17; 22:13; Jacob in ch. 46:1). By the time of Moses the practice of offering sacrifices was so well established that it passed easily into the religion of Yahweh, perhaps with the special assistance of Jethro, Moses' father-in-law (Ex. 18:12).[7] The later literature of the Old Testament shows that sacrifice and other sacred actions continued to play a vital role in Israelite religion so long as the Temple existed. With the centralization of worship at the Jerusalem Temple in the seventh century, sacrifices could not be performed anywhere else (II Kings 23:1–23).

In the Priestly tradition the sacrifices were the means par excellence for the worship of God in every respect. Chapters 1 to 7

of Leviticus specify in detail the types of offerings and sacrifices
included in Israelite religion, as well as all the requirements for
the proper performance of these rituals. In these codes holiness is
almost purely cultic, and one is struck by the concern expressed
here for ritual purity. It is as though no other avenue of approaching God existed and only through a precise procedure could
Israel hope to establish and maintain her relationship with Yahweh. We must recall, however, that these laws were accepted as
part of the covenant requirements, and as such were taken to be
an expression of the kind of response that God desired from his
people.

4. *Sacred persons.* Sacred actions were performed at sacred
places by sacred persons, the priests, who were men consecrated
to the LORD. The tribe of Levi was designated a priestly group
apparently quite early in Israel's history (see Num. 1:47–54;
ch. 3). Their status and duties are specified in these passages and
in additional descriptions in Ex., chs. 28; 30; 31. The ordination
of the priests was commanded by the LORD, according to Ex.,
ch. 29, and the account of the actual service of consecration is
recorded in Lev., ch. 8. The liturgical regulations of Lev., chs.
1 to 7, also contain instructions to the priests concerning their
performance of the sacrifices (see chs. 6:8 to 7:38).

Everything in the Old Testament concerning the office of the
priest presupposes his holiness as a man set apart for the service
of God. If we inquire as to the reason for the priest's being
specially qualified as a holy man, we find an answer primarily in
the understanding that those who are to be responsible for sacred
matters must themselves be set apart or sacred. We have already
seen that man's holiness is a derivative of God's, to the degree that
man participates in a positive relationship with God and avoids
the profane. The same is true of the priest to an even greater
extent. He must observe all the requirements of holiness so that
he can be sanctified for the duties of his office, handling sacred
objects and performing sacred actions in sacred places. His conduct and faithfulness to God's laws were expected to excel that
of other men (see Lev., ch. 21).

The other sacred persons in the Old Testament are prophets

and kings, and their holiness is of a different character from that of the priests. Whatever is sacred about these persons or about their offices is due solely to their association with God, as in the case of the priests. But the sacredness of the prophets came from their service as spokesmen of the divine word. For this function God had chosen them and set them apart, and they felt the divine vocation as an ordination fully commensurate with that of the priests (e.g., Amos 7:15; Isa., ch. 6; Jer. 1:4–10; Ezek., chs. 1 to 3). The kings of Israel, at least in the early Deuteronomic history, were also sacred persons who had been divinely selected and anointed. This is especially clear in the stories of Saul and David (I Sam. 10:1, 6; 16:13; 24:6; 26:11; II Sam. 1:14, 16). In the case of the prophets and kings, however, their sacredness did not entitle them to the same cultic rights possessed by the priests, nor did it prevent their being mistreated and at times even put to death.

5. *Sacred times.* Every sacred action takes place in sacred time. From one viewpoint, the performance of the action itself hallows the time in which it is performed. So general and abstract a concept as this, however, is never elaborated in the Old Testament, but we do have the recognition that certain special observances always take place at designated sacred times. Israel's religion came to be characterized to a considerable extent by the importance of these sacred festivals or holy days.

We have already mentioned the Passover as one of the earliest and most significant of such sacred occasions. It had been a primitive nomadic spring celebration of the birth of lambs, including the sacrificial offering and eating of lambs (Ex. 12:1–13), which later became an annual commemoration of the exodus from Egypt. The Passover season was thus one of Israel's most important sacred times, a celebration of God's goodness to his people.

At least three other annual sacred times are specified in the law (see Ex. 23:14–17; 34:18, 22 f.). The Feast of Unleavened Bread was originally an agricultural observance, associated with the end of the barley harvest in spring (Deut. 16:9). After the exodus this feast was connected with the seven days of the Passover season. Fifty days after the beginning of the Feast of Unleavened

Bread came Pentecost ("Fiftieth"), or the Feast of Weeks, another agricultural festival celebrating the first harvest of the wheat crop (Ex. 23:16). In the fall of each year was the festival called Sukkoth ("Booths"), or the Feast of Ingathering, especially of the grapes. The term "Booths" probably relates to the shelters erected in the fields during the time of harvesting (but see Lev. 23:42 f.). The New Year also was observed in the fall, and in later times a ten-day period of repentance was added following the first day of the year, ending with Yom Kippur, the solemn Day of Atonement (Lev., ch. 16).

In the postexilic period two additional holy days appeared. The Feast of Purim ("Lots") celebrates the deliverance of the Jews in Persia from their enemies, as described in The Book of Esther. The Feast of Hanukkah ("Dedication"), also called the Feast of Lights, occurs on the twenty-fifth of the Jewish month Kislev (November-December), and commemorates the rededication of the Jerusalem Temple by Judas Maccabaeus about 165 B.C. Additional times of fasting, penitence, prayer, and mourning are mentioned in the Old Testament, but without special historical associations.

Finally, the observance of the new moon, or the first of the month in the lunar calendar, seems to have been a common practice from early times (Num. 10:10; 28:11–15). Its origin may go back to the worship of the Mesopotamian moon god, Sin. The Sabbath, or seventh day of the week, came to be a very important sacred time for Judaism also. We do not know how this observance originated, although it was eventually attributed to God's command after the creation, according to the P account (Gen. 2:2 f.). Sabbath apparently was observed in Moses' time (see the Fourth Commandment, Ex. 20:8–11; cf. chs. 23:12; 34:21), and it has of course continued to be a significant occasion throughout the history of Israel's religion.

THE WORSHIP OF GOD

In the preceding discussion of God and the sacred we have chiefly stressed the specific aspects or features of the sacred in the structure of Israelite religion. We have been attempting to show how these sacred places, persons, times, and so on, actualized Israel's relationship with the Holy One in specific and concrete ways. As we have insisted before, all of this presupposes the sacredness of God and the possibility of man's being sanctified as a derivative of his closeness to God. What this amounts to, then, is that in religion, or in a more limited sense, in worship, the sacred quality possessed only by the Deity is transferred or imputed to man and to his objects and actions. We must keep in mind, however, that while God *is* holy, man only *becomes* holy, and that only in ways like those we have described above.

The worship of God in the Old Testament consists of the performance of many observances and the fulfillment of many requirements, as we have noted already. These ritualistic aspects of worship, detailed in the laws, were vital to Israel's religious life because they concretized for the common man the presence and power of God and of his control over every part of man's life. They were vital to the priest especially, for they provided the *raison d'être* of his office and of his personal existence. Moreover, the structure of worship helped to give form and purpose to the religion itself, marking it as separate from man's other activities, as well as from other religions, and helping it to survive through periods of stress and even of disaster.

But what do we learn about the nature of God from a study of Israel's religion? Some answers to this question have been given earlier in the chapter, and here we shall discuss only the idea of God's presence in worship. For Israel, there was no question of the personal presence of God in her religious experience. He had come into the national consciousness at supreme moments in her history, and he was present in a real sense in her everyday affairs. Israel's awareness of the immanence of God was heightened in worship, to be sure, but it was never lost sight of apart from worship, either.

In general, the language of the Old Testament always has to be taken as the language of worship when God is the object. God is never impersonal or abstract; rather, he is living and personal and present, especially when man draws closer to him in worship, in the experience of the sacred. At the same time, God transcends immediate experience. He is never contained in nor limited by his presence at a particular sacred time in a particular sacred place. He is Creator and Ruler of the world, and thus is quite independent of it. Yet he is not separated from the world, for he is constantly and everywhere present and at work in it. And it is in worship that his presence is most effectively realized in human experience.

Worship in the Old Testament is seen most acutely as a response to God's will and to what he had done for his people. This action-reaction theme is prominent in the law, the history, the prophets, and in the poetry of the Old Testament. Within this process, especially as it operates at the level of worship, there is a subsidiary or concomitant process at work. In worship, man not only reacts to God's action, whether in thanksgiving, repentance, or supplication, but also through his own actions he expects a reply from God. This pattern of petition and response is an essential element in Israelite religion. We note especially in the later cultic literature, in several psalms for example,[8] that plea and reply are prominent liturgical themes.

It is here, that is, in the postexilic Temple cultus, that priest and prophet seem to have joined forces for the first time in Israelite religion, although prophets may have participated in Temple ritual in a minor way even in preexilic times. Recent studies of the Old Testament psalms and prophetic writings have revealed the importance of the cultic prophet in Israel's worship, showing that ordinarily the prayer of petition in public worship was offered by the priest, and that the Temple prophet standing at his side then received and spoke the LORD's response. This research requires us to revise drastically the typical understanding of hostility and antithetical interests between priests and prophets in the Old Testament, and gives us new insight into the place of later prophets in Israelite worship.[9]

One further aspect of the worship of God must be mentioned here also. Worship has been seen as a reaction or response to God in which his "worth" is acknowledged and his sacredness realized. We have also said that worship is itself an action, sometimes done in expectation of a reply or response from God, but always done in obedience to the command and requirements of God. Another way of looking at this subject is to say that action or obedience is itself worship, since it ascribes worth or importance to the One who requires the action. Moreover, the Old Testament seems to say throughout that whatever man does that is in keeping with the divine will upholds the glory of God and is in itself a sacred action. The prophetic view can be understood in this way, even to the point of including man's duty toward his fellowman. It follows, therefore, that the worship of God may include not only the usual ritual actions, but also those responses to God's nature and will that in any way glorify him and his holiness.

ISRAEL'S RELIGION AND THE RISE OF JUDAISM

A study of the history of religion in the Old Testament shows successive stages of development, from preliterate concepts (animism, demonism, polytheism, etc.) to the tribal religion of the patriarchs to the high religion of Yahwism (including monotheism and prophetism), and finally to the postexilic religion called Judaism. There is, of course, no sharp division between these stages, for there was always some overlapping of ideas and practices, and no simple evolutionary process is to be seen at work here. One stage did not necessarily arise only from the preceding one, but frequently owed its development in part to other, even foreign, factors. Nor do the terms "preliterate," "tribal," "Yahwism," and "Judaism" represent all that was religiously important in each stage, for there was always present the fact of variety and disunity.

There is some value, however, in identifying successive developments in the history of Old Testament religion, for in this manner we are better able to understand the changing concepts of God and of Israel's place in the divine plan. The literature of the Old Testament is more meaningful also when we can relate it to a particular stage in Israel's religious history, although some of the collections (e.g., Psalms, Isaiah) and some of the literary divisions (e.g., the Pentateuch, Prophets) belong to more than one period.

So far as Judaism is concerned, it has long been known that during the period of some fifty years of exile in Babylonia (ca. 587–539 B.C.) a very definite transformation of Israelite religion took place. It is too much an oversimplification to say that Judaism was a product of the Babylonian exile, for the processes that lead to the stage in religious history where Judaism is recognizable had been in operation for centuries before. In other words, Judaism is incontrovertibly the offspring of Israelite religion in all its previous history. But the experience of the exile did bring about certain changes, some subtle and some obvious, in the religion of the Jews who were in Babylonia. And it was they, almost alone, who preserved and carried forward the ancient faith, albeit in a somewhat new and different form.

The Jews of the exile were forced to reevaluate their understanding of history and of God's specific plan for them. The eighth- and seventh-century prophets had been telling them that as the chosen people they were even more responsible to God, and that their failure to remain faithful to the covenant would eventually result in their destruction at the hands of nations whom God would himself employ for their punishment. Now it had happened, and another prophet, Second Isaiah, while assuring the exiled Jews that they would be restored, insisted that their place in history was to be understood as that of a Suffering Servant, in order to bring "light to the nations." This, plus Second Isaiah's strong monotheistic proclamation, gave postexilic Judaism a new or at least renewed basis for its religious thought.

At the same time, the Jerusalem priests in exile were at work attempting to preserve the older traditions of history, law, and worship. Much of the Priestly literature of the Old Testament comes from this time, and despite the loss of the Temple, and with it the possibility of continuing the sacrificial system, interest in such matters apparently never waned. When, therefore, the Jews were permitted by Cyrus of Persia to return to their homeland (see above, Ch. VII), the reestablishment of the Temple cultus (recorded in Haggai and Zechariah) and the promulgation of the Torah (recorded in Ezra-Nehemiah) moved to the center of the postexilic religion of Judaism. Other factors were at work also, including the rise of neonationalism, the appearance of the Wisdom Writings, the decline of prophecy, the development of Messianism and apocalypticism, and the continuing pressure of numerous external forces, political and religious, upon the restored Jewish community.

The importance of two of the leading figures in postexilic times, Ezra and Nehemiah, is somewhat difficult to assess. The accounts of their work in Jerusalem, probably in the late fifth and early fourth centuries, are undoubtedly based on historical fact, but tradition has played a large role in shaping the records as we now have them. It does seem likely that Ezra brought a Torah scroll to Jerusalem, sometime *after* Nehemiah had begun to carry out certain reforms there, and that this action inspired the people to renew their loyalty to God within the framework of the covenant. The work of Ezra and Nehemiah must have given a strong impetus to the developments within Judaism that had been taking place since the exile, especially to its exclusivistic tendencies.

Scholars have often been tempted to refer to postexilic Judaism as a religion of Temple and Torah. It is probably fair to say that the Jews did become the "People of the Book," but they must also be seen as the people of the covenant, or better perhaps, as the people of the LORD. When we examine the religious thought of Israel we find various themes and emphases at various periods, and these may range from pure monotheism to strict legalism to crude chauvinism, but we should never lose sight of the fact that for Israel, God was always central. Whatever may have been the glories or the imperfections of the religion of Israel, it never obscured the belief in God as Creator, Ruler, and Redeemer, the only God for Israel.

IX

God in Wisdom and Poetry

OLD TESTAMENT WISDOM LITERATURE AND POETRY

Some time after the Babylonian exile had ended, there began to appear in Judaism the written product of many centuries of thought and teaching by the wise men or sages of Israel. They represent an element in the development of the religion of the Old Testament that we have not previously encountered, although much of what the sages had to say was foreshadowed in the words of the prophets. Their understanding of God is, however, of great interest and importance for our survey and for a comprehensive view of Old Testament thought.

The wise men of Israel did not play a major public role, as did the prophets and priests, yet their words and ideas must have had great popular appeal. Essentially they were humanistic thinkers who were concerned with the common life of common men. They believed that the good life consisted of knowing what pleased God and men, and of living within the boundaries of common sense and moderation. They were not so much concerned with political or religious matters on a national scale as with the individual and the knowledge or wisdom he needed to live properly and prosperously.

In all probability there were sages in Israelite society from earliest times, although they do not appear as named individuals in any of the early stories or histories. Wisdom literature from Egypt dates at least to the beginning of the first millennium B.C., and sages from Edom and other nations near Israel were also prominent (see Prov. 30:1; 31:1; Job 1:1; 2:11). We can expect that such men existed in the community of Israel as well. According to Old Testament tradition, King Solomon was one of the wisest of all sages and the author of some three thousand proverbs (I Kings 4:29–34). A large number of sayings in the present book of Proverbs was later attributed to him, although their origin cannot be determined with much certainty. It is only in the post-exilic period that we begin to encounter identifiable persons and writings of the wisdom school, for it is in these later centuries that the Old Testament wisdom literature is to be dated.

The three Old Testament wisdom books are Proverbs, Job, and Ecclesiastes.[1] Portions of these books may well have been current for many centuries before being collected and recorded, but the present books were composed between about 500 and 200 B.C. A few of the psalms and certain isolated sayings in other Old Testament books also belong to the wisdom genre, but in this chapter we shall confine our discussion to the understanding of God in the three great books of wisdom just mentioned.

As for Old Testament poetry, we have observed before that much of the Old Testament, especially the prophetic books, was composed in poetic form. There are major sections of poetry, for example, in Gen., ch. 49; Deut., chs. 32 and 33; Judg., ch. 5; II Sam., chs. 22 and 23; Lamentations; The Song of Songs (Solomon); and in all the prophets. Proverbs and Job are also written almost entirely in poetry, as is about one third of Ecclesiastes. But the greatest collection of poetry in the Old Testament is the book of Psalms, and it is with the psalms as representative of Old Testament poetry that we shall be chiefly concerned later in this chapter.[2]

There is hardly any aspect of Israel's religion that is not included in the psalms. This magnificent collection of devotional poetry ranges over the whole spectrum of religious thought and practice, from the individual's prayers of thanksgiving, lamentation, and petition, to prophetic and royal psalms concerned with the nation's welfare. Composed by many different authors, and ranging in time from the tenth century to the fourth century B.C., these poems express the most profound feelings of religious faith;

feelings that were captured by gifted poets, and whose expression in the psalms made a major contribution to the development of Israel's religion and worship. The understanding of God in the psalms is varied and complex, yet it is possible to discover the underlying concepts and the major themes. This will be our task in the last section of this chapter on God in Old Testament wisdom and poetry.

THE WISDOM OF GOD

In most of the Old Testament the concept of God is shaped largely by the ideas of his power, righteousness, and holiness. As we would expect, however, the wisdom literature stresses God's knowledge, understanding, and wisdom. This does not mean that the rest of the Old Testament has overlooked these attributes of God. In Joshua, for example, some of the Israelites are reported to have cried out: "The Mighty One, God, the LORD! The Mighty One, God, the LORD! He knows; and let Israel itself know!" (ch. 22:22). This was in reply to a charge that they had built an altar in rebellion against Yahweh. The point here is that God knows the truth even when man cannot see it. The same idea of God's knowledge or insight is present in the statement in First Samuel that "the LORD sees not as man sees; man looks on the outward appearance, but the LORD looks on the heart" (ch. 16:7). The superiority of God's knowledge and insight to that of man is a significant part of his incomparable wisdom.

Elsewhere in the Old Testament the wisdom of God is assumed, and is often particularly associated with his control over history. Second Isaiah, for example, saw the divine wisdom in God's plans and thoughts for present and future events (see chs. 44:25; 46:10; 48:3, 5). God knew from the beginning what was to be, for in his wisdom he charted and guided the course of human history. The wisdom of God makes the wisdom of man seem foolish by comparison, and only through prophets and messengers can man know the words of wisdom that come from the divine source. Several of the psalms exalt the wisdom of God in similar terms, as well as encourage the good man to seek the ways of the LORD (see Ps.

1:6; 37:18; 44:21; 94:11; 103:14; 138:6). These psalms, or parts thereof, belong to the wisdom genre, as we observed in the preceding section.

When we turn to the wisdom books as such, it becomes obvious that the wisdom of God is their fundamental premise. In Hebrew the same terms for knowledge and wisdom that apply to man are used of God. In everything that is said, however, stress is laid upon the infinite superiority of God's wisdom over man's, as we noted in the texts from Joshua, First Samuel, and Second Isaiah. An entire section of The Book of Job (chs. 38 to 41; cf. 23:10) is taken up with this particular point, and is indeed one of the major theological ideas in Job. It is as though the author of Job was influenced by, or at least was in complete agreement with, the conviction expressed by Second Isaiah:

> For my thoughts are not your thoughts,
>   neither are your ways my ways, says the LORD.
> For as the heavens are higher than the earth,
>   so are my ways higher than your ways
>   and my thoughts than your thoughts.
>   (Ch. 55:8 f.)

We shall want to look further into these ideas in our discussion of Job later in this chapter.

A somewhat different stress on the nature of God's wisdom comes from Proverbs. There the wisdom of God, as it relates to man's existence, is essentially pragmatic. The sages who produced the greatly varied aphorisms, epigrams, and maxims of Proverbs were concerned first with man's ordinary life and with the guidance for successful living that could be found in the wisdom of God. Responsibility to the demands of God, plus correct and useful social or community behavior, stand out as major themes in this collection of wise sayings. In Proverbs we find also the understanding that the wisdom of God is seen in the Creation, and that the earth, the heavens, and the deeps all declare the wisdom of their Creator (Prov. 3:19 f.).

Ecclesiastes presents a still different idea of God's wisdom, although in this unusual collection of wisdom poetry and essays the concept of the inscrutable and transcendent nature of God is somewhat like that of Job. The author of Ecclesiastes approaches wisdom from a philosophical perspective, and by the use of reason attempts to apprehend the direction that man must take in relation to the divine will. The influence of Greek philosophy on this author, while not particularly relevant to his concept of God's wisdom, needs to be kept in mind if we are to arrive at the deeper meaning of this stimulating wisdom book.

THE BEGINNING OF WISDOM

The fear of the LORD is the beginning of knowledge;
fools despise wisdom and instruction.
(Prov. 1:7.)

The entire book of Proverbs, comprising several hundred individual poetic sayings, can be seen as an extended commentary on these lines. For in their program for man's best life, the sages looked to God as the supreme source of all knowledge and understanding, and in their own ways they sought to give in their teachings about the good life a practical application of the divine wisdom. Above all things they prized reasonable and enlightened behavior, and over and over they repeated the admonition that only fools would fail to follow the ways of wisdom and instruction.

We need to inquire at this point into the meaning of "the fear of the LORD" in the context of wisdom literature. We saw in the preceding chapter on Israelite religion that this phrase came out of the original awe or even terror experienced in the presence of deity, and that it was related to the attitude of worship. In Proverbs "the fear of the LORD" refers to the same attitude of reverence and obedience to God, but the saying quoted at the beginning of this section draws the further conclusion that in this attitude man has the prerequisite for beginning to become enlightened. This assertion is repeated in another proverb consisting of a parallel construction of the same idea stated in two ways:

The fear of the LORD is the beginning of wisdom,
and the knowledge of the Holy One is insight.
(Prov. 9:10.)

From passages such as this we learn that the wise men of Israel thought of wisdom as being revealed by God himself. Man is not able to fathom the sources of wisdom nor to acquire knowledge by his own efforts. The secrets of the world are in God's domain, and man cannot enter therein (see ch. 30:1–4). But God has given the principle of wisdom to man's mind, where it is apprehended in reason, common sense, and in obedience to the laws of God. God has also revealed the truth in his own words, and man should not presume to add to this truth (ch. 30:5 f.)

One of the most fascinating, and at the same time perplexing, aspects of the presentation of the wisdom idea in Proverbs is its personification. In chs. 1 to 9 the concept of Wisdom comes to life both as the preexistent principle or agent in Creation (ch. 8:22–31) and as an alluringly beautiful woman (chs. 1:20 f.; 8:4 f., 35 f.). The influence of Greek ideas is likely in this conception, although there was ample precedent also in the early Hebrew ideas of the Word and Spirit of God. This hypostatization of Wisdom should be looked upon not as a theological premise, but as a rhetorical or literary device. The sages did not intend to say that the being of God was somehow divided or plural; rather, they understood Wisdom to be identical with the Person of God, just as Word and Spirit were. There is only one God, but he has many aspects. Moreover, where Wisdom is personified as a beautiful woman, it is clearly for didactic purposes. The wise men were teachers as well as thinkers, and they used this method to make their instructions more vivid and forceful. The Wisdom of God should be attractive to men so that they will want to give up their foolish ways and follow the ways of God.

The ultimate purposes of the teaching of wisdom are stated specifically in the opening lines of Proverbs (ch. 1:1–6). These purposes are pragmatic and realistic, for the ideal of the wise man was an extremely practical one. Although there are some very lofty principles set forth in various proverbs, some of which show the influence of prophetic thought (e.g., chs. 15:8; 20:9; 21:3, 27; 28:13), the dominant theme is man's self-interest and the way to attain a happy and prosperous life. Altruism is conspicuously absent in the proverbs, and the level of prophetic ethics is never attained. Nor is any importance attached to the observation of ceremonial or cultic requirements. To serve and obey the LORD because it is profitable to do so is the theme most often repeated in Proverbs.

The scope of the wisdom teachings in Proverbs is immense, despite the limitations just mentioned. The whole range of man's common life is included in this book on the art of good living. There are words of wisdom concerning social behavior of all kinds, family relationships, business and professional matters, the responsibilities of those in authority, practical morality, and personal attitudes and manners. No list of topics or summary can do justice to this rich collection of materials, and the reader should peruse its contents carefully in order to see at first hand the wisdom contained therein.

One cannot help observing that in Proverbs there is much sound and useful advice that must have come from the best thinkers of the time, but that is still somewhat less than what we would like to believe is the wisdom of God. The fundamental assumption of Proverbs, as of much of the Old Testament for that matter, is that goodness will be rewarded and wickedness will be punished. There is, of course, some truth to this principle, but to many persons in this later period of Judaism the principle had become an inflexible rule. It had been applied with such severity, not only by the more traditional sages, but by prophets, priests, and historians as well, that it was coming to be questioned by a few thoughtful persons. One such person was the author of The Book of Job, whose profound insights and masterful writing made such an outstanding contribution to religious understanding. Before we go on to a consideration of the wisdom of God in Job, we shall need to examine briefly this principle of just retribution and its implications for Old Testament thought.

THE DOCTRINE OF JUST RETRIBUTION

It is correct to speak of the view that God rewards the good and punishes the evil as a "doctrine," because this view had come to be accepted almost without question as a basic principle by the thinkers and writers of the Old Testament. We are confronted by it in every major division of the literature. In the Torah or Pentateuch the Priestly writers have followed the principle of retribution quite consistently. Their narratives and laws reveal the conviction that punishment comes to men when they disobey the will of God, especially if they violate a regulation of the cultus. Sin can be removed or atoned for only through observance of the proper ritual requirements. Thus are good and evil defined in Priestly categories.

The Deuteronomic historians and prophets, as we have seen before (Chs. V, VI), found in their analysis of history, both in past events and in contemporary affairs, the justice of God at work. The world and human affairs did not just go along by chance or blind circumstance. God was always in control, and his will was exercised, especially in the framework of the covenant, to bless the faithful and upright and to curse the unfaithful and wicked. The historians and prophets agreed that the rule of God was just, and that man must conform to it. They saw in the wickedness and apostasy of Israel nothing but disaster, and when history brought defeat and ruin to the nation they accepted it as the sign of divine punishment.

It is not difficult to see how such an emphasis upon God as Lord of history and Ruler of the universe could lead to the doctrine of retribution. We must remember, however, that this was not some immutable, impersonal principle at work in the nature of things. It was the understanding of God as one who ruled over and cared for his people in a personal manner. He was living and acting among them, and he demanded their loyal response to him. Unfortunately, this causal understanding of God's actions became an essentially mechanical system, one that left little room for exceptions, even though the prophets in particular always insisted that man could turn back to God and be restored to his favor. Nevertheless, by the time of Job the emphasis seems to have fallen largely on the formula, "righteousness brings reward, and wickedness brings punishment," as a sort of orthodox rubric for assessing life's problems.

There was one problem, however, that the accepted point of view either failed to recognize or chose to ignore. The question of theodicy, or the justice of God, is raised when one puts the doctrine of divine retribution to the test in particular cases. If we admit that God is just, and that he acts justly in dealing out rewards and punishments to the righteous and the wicked respectively, then what can we say about the case of a righteous man who suffers some misfortune? We can answer the question as to why men suffer by saying that it is their just punishment for doing evil. But when we face the question as to why a *good* man suffers, then the answer does not come so readily. The system did not take into account this possibility, and could therefore only fall back lamely onto its usual pat answer that the good were rewarded and the wicked were punished. That this was an inadequate answer is shown in The Book of Job. And even though the case of Job may have been an unusual one, it was of sufficient importance to provide the central theme of one of the truly great books of all religious literature.

GOD AND MAN IN THE BOOK OF JOB

Few books in the Old Testament are so original as The Book of Job in their presentation of the being and action of God. Yet Job's insistence on the majesty of the Deity did not come as a completely new conception in Judaism, for prophets, poets, and historians had long before asserted the supreme Lordship of their God. What was new in Job was the conclusion reached in the author's poetic attempt to clarify the essential relationship of man to God in reference to a particular and extremely difficult human situation. This conclusion was then one of the truly original and important contributions of the wise men to Old Testament thought.

It is not necessary to retell the story of Job here. We should note, however, that the prose prologue (chs. 1 and 2) and epilogue (ch. 42:7–17) were taken from an ancient folktale about a good man who suffered with patience the misfortunes that God sent upon him, and who in the end was rewarded for this good-ness and loyalty. This story provided the setting for the long epic poem that is actually the heart of the book (chs. 3:1 to 42:6). The poet was an anonymous sage who lived probably in the fifth century B.C. He gave his work the form of a dialogue between Job and his three friends (chs. 3 to 31), concluding with the LORD's words to Job from the whirlwind (chs. 38:1 to 42:6). The speeches of a young man named Elihu (chs. 32 to 37) were added later by another poet.

The central theme of the poem of Job is the nature of the rela-tionship between man and God. One may say immediately that this is the main theme of the entire Old Testament for that matter, but in Job this relationship is put into a new dimension of thought. The author of Job did not rely upon an interpretation of history for his conception of the way that man may know and serve God. His insight was based upon a particular problem in human experience and the understanding of God that was given to him in reflecting upon this problem. However we may formu-late the problem faced by the man Job, it can be fully appreciated only within the greater context of man's total experience of God and his understanding of God's nature. Thus, in this sense, the story of Job is the story of all men, and it has something to say to the human condition in every age.

Subsidiary to the central theme of man's relationship to God are several more specific questions that have often been allowed to obscure the larger theme. The question of why a righteous man should suffer is clearly posed by the ancient story of Job, and a serious attempt to answer it in a meaningful way is given by the poet-sage. The suffering of the righteous raises the issue of theodicy, the justice of God in his dealings with men, although this issue is not discussed abstractly in the poem, but in reference to the special case of Job. These questions belong also to the subject of divine retribution, the traditional formulation of which we have noted above in connection with Proverbs. The author of Job was especially concerned to refute this traditional view, and the value of the book is to be measured in part by his success in doing so. Finally, the issues listed here also relate to a matter not directly dealt with in Job, namely, the problem of the origin of evil. Although no solution to this problem is offered in Job, or elsewhere in the Old Testament for that matter, it is a question that lurks in the background of the whole story of Job.

We may now summarize the argument of the poem and the author's conclusions. The righteous Job, having suffered the loss of all that was dear to him, and now afflicted with bodily suffering as well, laments his treatment and demands of God an explanation. His three friends repeatedly insist that God is just and that a good man will surely have health and long life. The wickedness of Job, therefore, must be great, and he should confess his sins and be healed. God's majesty and power are so far above man that man cannot expect to understand his ways. And the justice of God is sure: the wicked will perish, but the righteous will be saved. The speeches of Elihu reiterate these points with even greater stress on the idea of retribution, but without adding anything significantly new to the debate.

The climax of the entire work is reached in the discourse of Yahweh. He has, as it were, listened patiently to these arguments and to the demands of Job for an answer to his questions. Now he comes like a storm to overwhelm Job and to set at nought the whole lengthy argument. In matchless poetry the author presents God as the ineffable and sublime Creator whose ways can neither be challenged nor comprehended. God now asks the questions, and they are questions that Job (or man) cannot possibly begin to answer, for they belong to the hidden depths of God and of his creation. God is the Almighty, the Creator and supreme Ruler of all, and who is Job to defy God? The point is simply that God is God and man is man. Job finally admits that he is nothing in comparison with God, and that he was wrong to challenge God. He yields to God, and thus comes to an understanding of man's true relationship to his Creator, the relationship of unreserved trust, regardless of individual experience.

This solution to the problems raised by human experience, especially that of suffering, is a hard one, like some of the "hard sayings" of Jesus in the New Testament.[3] In rejecting the rigid formulation of the doctrine of divine retribution, Job offers no easy, pat answer with which to replace the traditional view. To say that all things are bound up in the mystery of God, and that man must accept whatever comes and continue to trust in God's wisdom and justice, is not an easy solution for man's problems, whether in the fifth century B.C. or in any other time. It is doubtful that Jews of the time of Job's author took readily to this difficult line of thought, although the book was sufficiently appreciated to be accepted as sacred Scripture.

In attempting to evaluate the contribution of the poet-sage who wrote Job to our understanding of God in the Old Testament, we must remember that the author began with traditional ideas about the nature and actions of God. He was the Creator, the Lord of history, the powerful and just Ruler of man and the universe, and the God whose transcendence and immanence were both necessary to his total being. The author of Job made a remarkable achievement in his emphasis upon both the sublime majesty of God and his profound involvement in man's destiny. Moreover, he advanced an understanding of God that clearly takes into account the limitations of human knowledge and insight. Man the creature must start from the point of his own weakness, admitting with Job that there is no logical or philosophical answer to his questions about God:

> Then Job answered the LORD:
> "I know that thou canst do all things,
>   and that no purpose of thine can be thwarted.
> 'Who is this that hides counsel without knowledge?'
> Therefore I have uttered what I did not understand,
>   things too wonderful for me, which I did not know."
>   (Ch. 42:1–3.)

What we are left with, then, is an almost mystical sense of the divine presence, of the ineffable nature of the divine-human encounter. This conclusion is saved from the obscurity of mysticism, however, by Job's profound awareness of the reality of God in human experience and of the faith required of man in response to God's presence in his life.

THE WISDOM OF GOD AND THE WISDOM OF MEN

When we turn to Ecclesiastes, the third Old Testament book of wisdom, we encounter a point of view entirely different from any other in the Old Testament. Men like the Second Isaiah and the author of Job had departed rather far from the traditional views of their time, the former by new insights into Israel's role in history, and the latter by a radical denial of the doctrine of retribution. But the author of Ecclesiastes expresses an understanding of God that is *sui generis* in Old Testament literature and that in some respects is closer to Greek than to Hebrew thought. He seems to have been a professional philosopher, a sage and teacher of about the third century B.C., whose ideas were collected in an unorganized manner in a book the title of which means something like "The Preacher."[4]

The essays or discourses in Ecclesiastes cover a wide range of subjects, but they all relate to the author's central concern with the meaning of life. His attempt to grasp the significance of human existence and the essence of the good life are based upon the use of reason. Like many of the Greek philosophers, this sage had rejected the so-called revelations of God that were the foundation of traditional religion, especially of his own Hebrew faith. Rather, he had applied his mind "to seek and to search out by wisdom all that is done under heaven" (Eccl. 1:13). Furthermore, he had tested or tried several ways of knowing absolute good (chs. 1:17; 2:1, 9, 12, 20 f.), but the inevitable conclusion to all of his research was that all was vanity, like a breath. He was convinced that man could neither change the world for the better nor achieve an understanding of the mysteries of existence by his own efforts.

> Vanity of vanities, says the Preacher,
> vanity of vanities! All is vanity.
> (Ch. 1:2.)

Much has been written about Ecclesiastes' pessimistic view of life, a view qualified only by his admission that man can enjoy a kind of temporal happiness, a day-to-day enjoyment of whatever pleasures he finds in life (chs. 2:24–26; 5:18–20; 9:2–12). What is of perhaps even greater significance, however, are the implications that his view has for an understanding of God. Instead of concentrating on the author's involvement with the lot of man, we shall want to discover what his ideas tell us about the nature of the God who is so often referred to in his discourses.

We have noted in The Book of Job the idea that the ways of God are too deep and hidden for man to comprehend, for man simply cannot participate in the fullness of divine knowledge and wisdom. Man can only accept and trust God. Ecclesiastes has come to a similar conclusion, and he does not hesitate to assert it in an extreme form. Unlike Job, who had experienced the reality of God in a direct, personal encounter, Ecclesiastes had little understanding of God as a concerned and compassionate Being. For him, God was the aloof and inscrutable Ruler of man and the universe. God was distant and essentially uninvolved in human affairs, and his rule was not determined by known standards of righteousness (chs. 8:10 to 9:1). Man's efforts to know and understand God were thus in vain (chs. 3:10 f.; 11:5), and man can do nothing to change the nature or course of things as God has determined them (chs. 3:1 f., 9, 14; 7:14).

Despite this skepticism, the author of Ecclesiastes did not think to question the existence of God or the reality of God's control over all things. His heterodoxy did not lead him to atheism, but rather to an agnosticism with regard to the ways of Deity. His religious stance contrasts sharply, of course, with that of other Old Testament thinkers. The belief that God is knowable in history and in human affairs, and that his righteousness and justice are revealed in these events, is fundamental to the prophets and historians in particular. But the experience and reflection of Ecclesiastes have brought him to a different conclusion, and at this point he is also exceptional in that his wisdom does not build upon the insights of the prophets.

Although the meaning of existence is hidden from man, there is a religious obligation that the wise man will fulfill, according to Ecclesiastes. God is worthy of man's reverence ("fear" in ch. 5:7), and wisdom decrees that a man sincerely fulfill his formal obligations to the God of heaven (ch. 5:1–6). His advice concerning prayer and the payment of religious vows urges that these acts be done in moderation and with a sense of detachment, and not as the religious fools whose piety is ignorant and overly enthusiastic.

Finally, we should note that many of the words and ideas of this wise man must have been quite offensive to the pious and orthodox Jews of his time. How, then, did the book find its way into the canon of sacred Scripture? Perhaps the idea that it was written by Solomon made it more acceptable, and it may also have been supported by other influential sages. More important, however, is the fact that it was partially edited or revised by the insertion of numerous statements that tended to modify or even deny some of the more troublesome passages.[5] Thus the reflections of an original though unorthodox thinker were not allowed to stand unchallenged by the pious community, but were brought into closer harmony with the traditional understanding of the Old Testament God.

The God of Old Testament Poetry

In order that the title of this section not mislead the reader, let us say at the outset that to speak of the God of Old Testament poetry does not imply that somehow the poets held a unique concept of the God of Israel. The view of God contained in Psalms, which we shall take as representative of the Hebrew poetic tradition, accords completely with the general understanding of the God of Israel's history and faith that has appeared thus far in our study, outside of the wisdom literature. In other words, the psalmists also looked upon Yahweh as Creator, Lord of history, Redeemer of mankind, and Holy One of Israel. But it is the *personal* quality of God in Israel's experience that the psalmists understood and expressed most effectively. Thus the contribution that these poets made has to do with their special approach to God as the personal object of man's deepest religious feelings.

The psalms express Israel's emotional response to God, rather than a reflective or thought-out perspective on God's being and activities. The language of poetry is emotive and symbolic, not bound by rigid canons of historical or theological interpretation, but giving free rein to the most profound hopes, fears, and aspirations of the religious instinct. In these poetic songs of devotion God is exalted in ways that prose, even of the finest quality, cannot match.

A brief survey of the types of psalms that have been gathered into the remarkable and diverse collection called the book of Psalms will help us to sense something of the wide range of religious feeling they represent.[6] Careful analysis of types and groups of psalms according to their original use and themes has revealed a large number of categories into which they may be classified. In general, however, the psalms may be designated as being intended for either private or public devotional use. In the category of psalms for private worship there are those appropriate to the Temple and those which might be used elsewhere. The psalms suitable for public worship are almost all related to the Temple cultus, but may be distinguished as those used by the whole worshiping community and those reserved particularly for special persons or events.

A few examples from these general categories will suffice to illustrate the variety of types. Individuals wishing to express thanksgiving to a gracious God would find the words of Ps. 66 very helpful. An individual wishing to present a petition to God might ask for help against his enemies (Ps. 5), or for vindication of his innocence (Ps. 26), or he might even lament his misfortunes (Ps. 22). The most personal expressions of piety, however, are found in those psalms which originally came out of private rather than public piety. Such a psalm is the prayer of repentance in Ps. 51. The ineffable and cosmic presence of God in one individual's experience is beautifully stated in Ps. 139, a hymn of praise with monotheistic overtones. Psalm 91 expresses a personal confidence in God's providential care, and in Ps. 23 there is an unexcelled expression of the meaning of profound fellowship with God. These are but a few examples chosen from the many hymns of private devotion used in the Temple and elsewhere.

The psalms composed for and used in the rituals of corporate worship in the Temple give us perhaps our best view of the religious poets' understanding of the God of Israel. As we attempted to underscore in the preceding chapter, the Temple cultus was an extremely important part of Israel's religious life. The act of going to the sacred Temple area, especially at the times of the three great annual festivals, was accompanied by the singing of psalms such as those called "songs of ascents" (Ps. 120 to 134). These "pilgrim songs" were sung as the worshipers actually made their way up the Temple hill. Once in the holy place the hymns varied according to the occasion. For example, Ps. 65 and 67 give thanks for the harvest, and Ps. 81 was used for New Year celebrations. The so-called "enthronement psalms" (Ps. 47; 68; 93; 96 to 99) may also have been used to celebrate the enthronement of Yahweh as King in the course of the New Year rituals.

A number of psalms used in the Temple cultus originally related to a special person or event, notably the king and certain royal occasions. Psalms 2; 18; 20; 21; 45; 72, the "royal psalms," were composed for specific ceremonies, a royal wedding, a victory in battle, or the coronation of the king. It is not likely that the community as a whole was present at these occasions, although they were publicly celebrated in the Temple in most cases.

In all of these poems the mood of worship is intensely felt, for they attribute the significance of what is being said and done to the presence of God in his holy Temple or in the personal lives of individuals. The psalms in this respect reinforce the religious feeling of the group or the individual that life's most significant moments are those that are sanctified by personal communion with God. This is the view of matters as we look at the human side of religious experience. What more can the psalms tell us about God himself, as seen through the poetic expression of faith?

A list of specific ideas and feelings about God compiled from the psalms would be long and not necessarily helpful. Most of the items on such a list would be quite familiar as statements about God's goodness, kindness, righteousness, providence, power, and universality. The psalmists do not contribute any particularly new insights into the being of God or his work among men and in the universe. The experience of communion with God tends to override all expressions of the nature of deity and to give to the book of Psalms the quality of profound devotional literature.

We may conclude, therefore, that the God of Old Testament poetry is the God of Old Testament law, history, and prophecy understood in the context of worship and expressed in the rhythms, imagery, and metaphors of poetry. The important thing is that in the poetry of Psalms, God is living and accessible to the devout worshiper, in the privacy of his own meditation as well as in the great ceremonies conducted in the Temple. The God of the Old Testament is always personal, and nowhere more so than in the poetry of Psalms.

X

God of the Covenant: Old and New

It may seem somewhat unusual in a book on the Old Testament understanding of God to leave until the last chapter so important an idea as that of the covenant. Some scholars have insisted that the covenant is *the* central and dominating theme of Old Testament thought, although our survey of the ideas of God in the Old Testament does not fully support that conclusion. We have, however, referred to the covenant concept at several points in earlier chapters, and its significance has been fully appreciated in our attempt to discover the Hebrew or Israelite view of God.

One reason for returning to the idea of the covenant God in this chapter is suggested by the second half of the chapter heading, "Old and New." Our position is that the covenant idea is the essential bridge between the Old and New Testaments.[1] The God of the two Testaments, or Covenants, is of course the same deity, but his redeeming acts in history are most significantly related to the two Covenants, Old and New. Furthermore, it is correct to say that historically the Old Covenant leads directly to the New, and that the New Covenant is undeniably based upon the Old.

We have said that even though the covenant concept occupies an important place in Old Testament thought, it is not exclusively the dominating idea, and it would be misleading to insist that the entire Old Testament is centered about this idea alone. It does provide a vital link between the two Testaments, however, and since our intention in this chapter is also to review what we have discovered of the Old Testament understanding of God, the covenant concept is a useful vehicle for such a review as well.

THE COVENANT GOD OF THE OLD TESTAMENT

The idea of a covenant or compact between God and man appears as early as the stories of Adam and Noah. Whether the idea was originally present in these primeval stories, or was read back into them in the light of later covenants, is another matter. Certainly the possibility of early man's making an agreement with his god is very strong, but the importance of the Abrahamic and Mosaic covenants suggests that these later agreements dominated even the earlier traditions about the ancestors of Israel.

Perhaps the most important result of the idea of Yahweh as the covenant maker was the identification of all the gods of the fathers with Yahweh. There can be little doubt that the Hebrew patriarchs knew and worshiped several deities (Ch. I), and that the unification of these gods occurred as part of the theological and literary processes in Israel's reflection upon the Mosaic era. The E stratum in Exodus states very clearly that Yahweh was known by the fathers, but only under the name El Shaddai, not Yahweh. The J tradition throughout the Pentateuch, of course, believed that God was known as Yahweh from the creation of the world (Ch. II).

A very important covenant was made by God with Abraham, involving significant promises for Israel's entire future. We shall consider these promises, as well as the concomitant obligations, in the next section, but here we must note the centrality of the covenant made through Moses. In this covenant God's election of Israel is fundamental, giving substance to the idea of the chosen people, which is in turn reflected in the stories of the patriarchs. The entire history of Moses and his prophetic role is set within the context of election and covenant (Ch. II). Moses did not discover Yahweh. On the contrary, Yahweh sought out and chose Israel as his special people, for reasons that the Old Testament writers, as in Deuteronomy, could only believe had to do with God's love and grace, not with any merit on Israel's part. The covenant God, coming into history to reveal his divine will for his people, gave Israel both the foundation and the *raison d'être* of her life as the covenant community.

The subsequent history of the people of God was written under the impress of the concept of the covenant God. The very essence of man's relationship to his Creator was bound up in the conviction that there were continuing bonds between Yahweh and his people. History writers did not need to search long for evidence of these bonds. In their view God acted in historical moments to carry out his divine scheme of events. Thus he had directed Abraham to Canaan, delivered Israel from Egypt, given the Law to Moses, led Joshua in his conquest of Canaan, raised up judges, appointed kings, and blessed, judged, and chastised Israel continually throughout her generations. Her prophets did not lose sight of the meaning of covenant responsibility (Chs. V, VI), and their words more than once attempted to recall Israel to the requirements of loyalty and obedience to the God of the covenant.

There were moments, such as the fall of Israel and Judah's exile in Babylonia, that must have seriously shaken Israel's faith in the covenant relationship. But there were still prophets to remind her that these events belonged to God's larger plan of redemption and that her destiny was still under his control (Ch. VII). After the exile, and with the return of Israel to a relatively stable life in her own land, the covenant idea was less pronounced. A concern for the law and the requirements of religion (Ch. VIII) began to take first priority in the community's consciousness. These concerns belonged to the covenant relationship also, but the emphasis came to be upon legalistic fulfillment rather than upon the ideal of covenant life as the prophets had described it. The only voices raised in opposition to the almost mechanical view of divine retribution that had developed by this time were those of a few thoughtful sages, such as the author of Job. They challenged the notion that the covenant God always acted in an arbitrary manner, and they attempted to show that man's acceptance of God's will and his faith in God's righteousness required more than just a glib mouthing of the old formulas of covenant religion (Ch. IX).

Both Judaism and Christianity have tended to elaborate an institutional expression of the covenant. In the Old Testament we have seen this expression in its most characteristic form as the "religion" of Israel. From a sociological point of view religion is to be studied as one aspect of human culture, and indeed this can be a very useful endeavor. What the sociologist may fail to recognize, however, is that religion always arises from some sort of transcendental experience that lies behind the facade of institutional forms. Thus, in the Old Testament, the covenant faith of Israel is basic to, and in many ways more significant than, the religion that grew from it. This is one of the reasons why we have chosen in this book to concentrate upon the fundamental Old Testament ideas of God rather than upon the history of Israel's religion.

OBLIGATIONS AND PROMISES IN THE OLD COVENANT

From the beginning of time the dual nature of the covenant relationship had been made explicitly clear. God offered to man all that is involved in a relationship with the sovereign Deity, while man agreed to accept the responsibilities that went with such a sacred alliance. In the case of Abraham, for example, the patriarch was required to go to a strange land at God's direction, to obey the commands of his Lord, even up to the sacrifice of his only son, and to trust in the divine purpose even when its meaning was most obscure to him. In return, God promised to Abraham a land of his own, a mighty nation from his seed, and a blessing through him to all mankind (Ch. I).

For most of the Old Testament the covenant obligations laid upon Israel by God are identified with the Law or Torah of Moses. The Old Covenant is essentially a covenant of law, that is, one in which Israel's responsibility to God is best summed up in the legal standards of the community, at least from the Priestly point of view. For this reason, the story of the great theophany and covenant-making experience at Sinai quickly becomes an account of the giving of the Law (Ch. II). In this account, especially in Exodus, but also in Leviticus and Deuteronomy, centuries of judicial thought and practice are brought together in one moment of time and given new and lasting significance as Israel's part of the agreement made at this time with the God of the covenant. From this moment Israel became the people of the Torah, a responsibility that she was never permitted to forget, and that has to a remarkable extent been characteristic of her religion to this day.

There were promises also, however, that lightened what could have been the terrible burden of the covenant Law. Yahweh was to be the God of Israel, as he had been since the days of Abraham, and this meant that she would be the recipient of his guidance, his protection, and his deliverance. And Yahweh more than fulfilled his part of the contract. Did he not deliver Israel out of bondage in Egypt? Was he not always before them during the trying years in the wilderness? And did he not lead them victoriously into the Land of Canaan to possess it as their own? The blessings of God upon his people were thus historically recounted by Old Testament prophets, poets, and historians.

In the theme of promise and fulfillment there is strong emphasis upon the covenant relationship. The promise had been made in the covenant with Abraham that his descendants would become a great nation and would possess their own land (Ch. I). The historians and editors of the Old Testament, principally in the Hexateuch, traced this promise through Israel's early history and discovered its fulfillment in the conquest of Canaan. To this end Yahweh had become the God of war, to lead Israel in strategy and action as she accomplished her military victories in Canaan (Ch. III). But this was not enough. Initial possession of the land did not guarantee continuing security, and so through the difficult days of the Judges, God kept the covenant as time and again he rescued the people from troubles of their own making. Israel suffered when she failed in covenant loyalty and worshiped other gods. God delivered her when she turned back in faithfulness to him (Ch. III).

God's promise to Israel came to fruition also in the establishment of the nation. There were doubts and difficulties in the institution of the kingship, but the prevailing view was that the first kings had been chosen by Yahweh himself to strengthen the covenant community and to make it a true nation (Ch. IV). A secondary covenant with David and his descendants on the throne of Judah seemed to be reassurance that God had chosen this means of keeping his original covenant promises. God himself was King and Ruler over Israel, and increasingly over all nations and the entire universe, and the history of his relationship with his subjects was clearly one of covenant-making and covenant-keeping. As the prophets continually reminded her, however, the covenant remained in effect only so long as Israel lived in covenant faithfulness to her God.

WHEN COVENANT FAITHFULNESS IS FORGOTTEN

The judgment upon ancient Israel as a people who failed to keep their covenant with God is not solely that of later Christian interpretation. The Old Testament itself pronounced that judgment, as we have seen most forcefully expressed in the prophetic books, wherein God's condemnation of Israel is stated in no uncertain terms. Even in the wilderness Israel could not completely turn away from idols, and once in Canaan the problem was simply exacerbated by contact with Baalism on all sides. The entire history of the period of the Judges was written as a story of repeated apostasy on Israel's part, always followed by divine deliverance when the people turned back to Yahweh. The early prophets of Israel, notably Elijah and Elisha, fought desperately to save the Northern Kingdom from the pitfalls of Baal religion (Ch. V). They succeeded temporarily, but they could not erase the ever-present tendency toward idolatry in Israel's religious life.

In the earliest days of the monarchy there seemed to have been less difficulty with this problem of apostasy. Despite its imperfections and liabilities the new system of government had brought unity and stability of a sort to the tribes of Israel, and loyalty to Yahweh was apparently relatively high during the days of Saul, David, and Solomon (Ch. IV). By the time of the first great prophets, however, not even a strong monarchical system[2] could save the two Kingdoms from the inevitable consequences of disloyalty to God and the covenant. The eighth-century prophets spoke a message in this regard that said essentially these four things:

1. All Israel has sinned and broken the covenant by worshiping other gods.
2. Israel's ethical shortcomings indicate lack of obedience to the just and righteous God.
3. God will punish and destroy Israel for her disloyalty and disobedience.
4. Israel's only hope of restoration is to turn from sin and idolatry and to return to Yahweh in covenant faithfulness.

Prophets such as Hosea, Amos, Isaiah, and Micah judged their times from their own peculiar perspectives, but they spoke as one in their interpretation of history and of what happens when covenant faithfulness is forgotten (Ch. VI). Jeremiah and Ezekiel echoed these views, and living at the very moment of Judah's destruction, they were able to comment with special insight upon the people's failure. The disappearance of the nation as a viable entity also encouraged these two spokesmen to suggest that a true relationship with God, indeed a completely new covenant, must be established by the individual, not just by the community.

Among the later prophets, Second Isaiah made the most significant contributions with his insistence upon explicit monotheism, his message of comfort to the exiled Jews, and his reinterpretation of the role of God's people as a Servant to the world (Ch. VII). This prophet was very much aware of the requirements of the covenant and the results of failure to keep covenant loyalty. But his view was turned toward the future rather than the past, and he believed that through her experience Israel could better serve God's purpose, not as the chosen people exclusively, but as a chosen Servant through whom the covenant with God might be opened to all people. We shall consider this concept more fully below in the discussion of the new covenant idea.

Other postexilic prophets spoke as they understood the words of God, but there was little concern with the covenant as such in their messages (Ch. VII). Haggai, Zechariah, and Malachi were most involved with the immediate needs of the rebuilding of the community in Jerusalem, founded to be sure upon the assumption of a continuing covenant with Yahweh. The words of Joel seemed to deny any view of the covenant as open to people other than the Jews, whereas in Jonah the unrestricted grace and forgiveness of Yahweh is preached. The Book of Daniel focuses upon the very real problems of loyalty to God and to the Law in times of persecution and distress, arguing effectively that faithfulness to all aspects of the covenant will result in God's blessing and protection, and eventually in victory over all the forces of evil.

GOD'S PROMISE OF A NEW COVENANT

The failure of Israel to remain faithful to Yahweh in terms of her covenant responsibilities eventually led some of her religious leaders to conceive the idea of a new covenant. The old covenant, originally made through Moses and subsequently renewed on a national basis by Joshua (Josh. 24:1–28), Josiah (II Kings 22:1 to 23:30), and Ezra (Neh., ch. 9), had broken down again and again, not so much because of imperfections within the covenant arrangement itself, but as a result of the weaknesses and failures of the people. Thus, to some at least, the only hope lay in the direction of an entirely new covenant relationship.

The first suggestion of the possibility of a new covenant with the LORD came from the eighth-century prophets who could look beyond Israel's doom to a day of restoration and a renewed relationship with her God. Hosea, perhaps speaking eschatologically, foresaw the LORD making a covenant "on that day," one that would have universal implications and would be characterized by the people's betrothal to the LORD in righteousness, justice, steadfast love (chesed), mercy, faithfulness, and knowledge (Hos. 2:16–20). Other prophets, including those of later centuries, shared this view and expressed it in their own terms (cf. Isa. 11:6–9; Micah 7:18–20; Ezek. 34:25–31). Prophecies of Israel's restoration and glorious future generally presuppose a new, or at least a renewed, covenant, but typically without explicit reference to it.

Jeremiah is usually credited with the most specific and significant statement of the new covenant concept. In one of his earlier pronouncements this great prophet had insisted on the requirement of faithfulness to the old covenant, using the phrases common to such pronouncements elsewhere in the Old Testament: "Cursed be the man who does not heed the words of this covenant which I commanded your fathers when I brought them out of the land of Egypt, from the iron furnace, saying, Listen to my voice, and do all that I command you. So shall you be my people, and I will be your God" (ch. 11:3–4; cf. ch. 7:23).

In other passages, however, the prophet sets his hope of a better relationship between God and Israel into a futuristic context, either after return from exile (Jer. 24:7; 32:38–40) or in the ideal age to come (ch. 30:21 f.). But this hope was most dramatically expressed in an oracle that was to become crucial for later thought on the new covenant. This oracle is of such importance that we must quote it in its entirety: "Behold, the days are coming, says the Lord, when I will make a new covenant with the house of Israel and the house of Judah, not like the covenant which I made with their fathers when I took them by the hand to bring them out of the land of Egypt, my covenant which they broke, though I was their husband, says the Lord. But this is the covenant which I will make with the house of Israel after those days, says the Lord: I will put my law within them, and I will write it upon their hearts; and I will be their God, and they shall be my people. And no longer shall each man teach his neighbor and each his brother, saying, 'Know the Lord,' for they shall all know me, from the least of them to the greatest, says the Lord: for I will forgive their iniquity, and I will remember their sin no more" (Jer. 31:31–34).

This promise is essentially eschatological, as the phrases "Behold, the days are coming" and "after those days" indicate. It includes the two Kingdoms, Israel and Judah,[3] but departs from tradition by implicitly rejecting the old covenant, now broken, and projecting an entirely different basis for the new relationship. The law of the Lord will be written, not on stone tablets, but upon the hearts of God's people (cf. ch. 32:38–40). In those days also the knowledge of God will be common to all men, for God will forgive them and erase the memory of their sin, thus restoring them to a holy or sacred relationship with him. The deep concern for the individual's relationship with God, discussed in a different context in Ch. VI above, is also present here.

We cannot be sure what impression this oracle may have made upon the people of Jeremiah's time. It does not appear to have been of great significance in sparking a religious reform or in persuading the people in general that the way of the law must give place to the way of the heart. Israel's history shows that she was ready to *renew* the old covenant from time to time, but to *replace* the old covenant with a new one seems to have been unthinkable to most of the people. The old covenant, with all its promises and obligations, has never been abrogated, so far as Judaism is concerned, and it has been largely responsible for holding the religious community of Jews together for some three thousand years. For Judaism, the seeds of the new are always present in the old, which is ever self-renewing and able to meet the changing spiritual needs of each new generation.

A new religious community appeared, however, believing that the promises of Jeremiah and other prophets were fulfilled in the life and death of a man who stood firmly within the old tradition and who probably did not intend to depart from it. Jesus of Nazareth was thoroughly Jewish, and so far as we know, he remained loyal throughout his life to the laws and ideals of the old covenant. But among his followers there were some who came to believe that a New Age had been inaugurated by the prophet from Galilee. Their experiences at the time of his crucifixion and resurrection, reinforced by events during the weeks immediately thereafter, convinced them that he was indeed the Man of God through whom a new relationship had been established. The people of the new covenant were at first Jews only, but it was soon understood that God intended that the covenant be open to men of all nations (Matt. 28:18–20; Luke 24:45–47; cf. Mark 16:15). Thus in Christianity the God of the covenant continued his redemptive purpose in history, not turning away from the old, but turning it toward the future and giving it a new and universal meaning.

With the appearance of the idea of a new covenant our survey of the Old Testament understanding of God comes to an end.

We have encountered in the foregoing pages most of the major ideas about God contained in the Old Testament, and we have tried to keep in mind that this great anthology of Israel's religious literature is a testament of her faith. It is not a work of systematic theology, and we cannot emphasize too strongly that we really do not know very much about how the Old Testament writers *thought*. The Old Testament is essentially confessional, not propositional; it is a response to events, to what Israel believed that God said and did in a special relationship with them as his people. They did not primarily reflect upon the conceptual meaning of his words and actions; rather, in the Old Testament we see revealed the living community of the faithful, which is something more than the product of intellectual and theological speculation. If we are to appreciate this insight, and to approach an understanding of God in Old Testament terms, we must do so in humility and in full awareness of our limitations as people of the twentieth century. We do not find it easy to become involved in the language and thought and faith of the pre-Christian centuries, and the meaning and relevance of the Old Testament for our contemporary world is not always clear. In this book we have not attempted to make the Old Testament "speak to our day" by simplifying its message or by trying to force its ideas into modern categories and to relate them to present-day problems and needs. Nevertheless, we remain fully convinced that much of the Old Testament continues to have something vital and significant to say to all of us today, and we hope that the reader will endeavor to find that something for himself in his study of the Old Testament.

Selected Bibliography

Albright, William F., *From the Stone Age to Christianity: Monotheism and the Historical Process,* 2d ed. The Johns Hopkins Press, 1957.

Anderson, Bernhard W. (ed.), *The Old Testament and Christian Faith.* London: SCM Press, Ltd., 1964.

——— *Understanding the Old Testament.* Prentice-Hall, Inc., 1957.

Baab, Otto J., *The Theology of the Old Testament.* Abingdon Press, 1949.

Bentzen, Aage, *King and Messiah.* London: Lutterworth Press, 1955.

Bright, John, *The Kingdom of God.* Abingdon Press, 1953.

Buber, Martin, *The Prophetic Faith,* tr. by Carlyle Witton-Davis. The Macmillan Company, 1949.

Buck, Harry M., *People of the Lord: The History, Scriptures, and Faith of Ancient Israel.* The Macmillan Company, 1966.

Burrows, Millar, *An Outline of Biblical Theology.* The Westminster Press, 1946.

Davidson, A. B., *The Theology of the Old Testament.* Charles Scribner's Sons, 1904.

Dentan, Robert C., *Preface to Old Testament Theology,* rev. ed. The Seabury Press, Inc., 1963.

Eichrodt, Walther, *Theology of the Old Testament,* Vol. I (The Old Testament Library), tr. by J. A. Baker. The Westminster Press, 1961.

Harrelson, Walter, *Interpreting the Old Testament*. Holt, Rinehart and Winston, Inc., 1964.

Heschel, Abraham J., *The Prophets*. Harper & Row, Publishers, Inc., 1962.

Hyatt, J. Philip, *Prophetic Religion*. Abingdon-Cokesbury Press, 1947.

Jacob, Edmund, *Theology of the Old Testament*. Harper & Brothers, 1958.

Johnson, Aubrey R., *The Cultic Prophet in Ancient Israel*. Cardiff: University of Wales Press Board, 1944.

Kaufmann, Yehezkel, *The Religion of Israel: From Its Beginnings to the Babylonian Exile*, tr. and abridged by Moshe Greenberg. The University of Chicago Press, 1960.

Knudson, Albert C., *The Religious Teaching of the Old Testament*. Abingdon Press, 1918.

Köhler, Ludwig, *Old Testament Theology*, 3d ed. The Westminster Press, 1958.

Leslie, Elmer A., *Old Testament Religion*. Abingdon-Cokesbury Press, 1936.

Minear, Paul S., *Eyes of Faith: A Study in the Biblical Point of View*. The Westminster Press, 1946.

Mowinckel, Sigmund, *He That Cometh*, tr. by G. W. Anderson. Oxford: Basil Blackwell & Mott, Ltd., 1956.

Muilenburg, James, *The Way of Israel: Biblical Faith and Ethics*. Harper & Brothers, 1961.

Napier, B. Davie, *From Faith to Faith*. Harper & Brothers, 1955.

North, Christopher R., *The Old Testament Interpretation of History*. London: The Epworth Press, Publishers, 1946.

—— *The Suffering Servant in Deutero-Isaiah*, 2d ed. London: Oxford University Press, 1956.

Oesterley, W. O. E., and Robinson, T. H., *Hebrew Religion*, 2d ed. The Macmillan Company, 1937.

Orlinsky, Harry M., *Ancient Israel*. Cornell University Press, 1954.

Pedersen, Johannes, *Israel: Its Life and Culture*, Vols. I–II, III–IV. London: Oxford University Press, 1926–1940.

Robinson, H. Wheeler, *Inspiration and Revelation in the Old Testament*. Oxford: The Clarendon Press, 1946.

—— *The Religious Ideas of the Old Testament*. Charles Scribner's Sons, 1913.

Rowley, H. H., *The Biblical Doctrine of Election*. London: Lutterworth Press, 1964.

—— *The Faith of Israel*. The Westminster Press, 1957.

—— *The Servant of the Lord*. London: Lutterworth Press, 1952.

—— *Studies in Old Testament Prophecy*. Charles Scribner's Sons, 1950.

Sandmel, Samuel, *The Hebrew Scriptures*. Alfred A. Knopf, Inc., 1963.

Smart, James D., *The Old Testament in Dialogue with Modern Man*. The Westminster Press, 1964.

Snaith, Norman H., *The Distinctive Ideas of the Old Testament*. The Westminster Press, 1946.

von Rad, Gerhard, *Old Testament Theology*, Vols. I and II, tr. by D. M. G. Stalker. Edinburgh and London: Oliver & Boyd, Ltd., 1962–1965.

Vriezen, Theodorus C., *Outline of Old Testament Theology*, tr. by S. Neuijen. Oxford: Basil Blackwell & Mott, Ltd., 1958.

Welch, Adam C., *Prophet and Priest in Old Israel*. Oxford: Basil Blackwell & Mott, Ltd., 1953.

Wright, G. Ernest, *God Who Acts*. London: SCM Press, Ltd., 1952.

—— *The Old Testament Against Its Environment*. Henry Regnery Company, 1950.

Notes

CHAPTER I. God in Early Hebrew Thought

1. The "four-document hypothesis" includes these sources: J (from the use of Jehovah or Yahweh), a tenth-century Judean document; E (from Elohim, "God"), a ninth- or eighth-century Israelite document; D (Deuteronomy), a seventh-century Judean document; P (Priestly), sixth-century material prepared by Jews in Babylonian exile. This hypothesis must be used with great caution, however, especially in the light of what recent research reveals concerning the preliterary stages of the history of Old Testament traditions.

2. On the differences between later Yahwism and Canaanite Baalism, see below, Ch. V.

3. Many of these ancient stories are translated and discussed in Samuel Noah Kramer (ed.), *Mythologies of the Ancient World* (Quadrangle Books, Inc., 1961).

4. This statement is based on a definition given in Millar Burrows, *An Outline of Biblical Theology* (The Westminster Press, 1946), p. 115.

5. The word *nephesh*, "breath," has a meaning similar to that of *ruach* and is used in at least one important passage (Gen. 2:7) with the meaning of "life" or "spirit." An excellent treatment of these ideas may be seen in Johannes Pedersen, *Israel: Its Life and Culture*, Vols. I–II (London: Oxford University Press, 1926), pp. 99–181.

6. This theory of tribal deities was carefully worked out by Albrecht Alt in *Der Gott der Väter* (Stuttgart: Kohlhammer, 1929), but it is still disputed by some Old Testament scholars.

CHAPTER II. The God of Moses

1. The theory of multiple sources in the Pentateuch (above, p. 28, n.1) is too complex for treatment here. For a detailed survey, see

Cuthbert A. Simpson, "The Growth of the Hexateuch," *The Interpreter's Bible,* ed. by George A. Buttrick *et al.,* Vol. I (Abingdon-Cokesbury Press, 1952), pp. 185–200.

2. The Priestly tradition in Ex. 6:2–3 informs us that God was known to Abraham, Isaac, and Jacob as "God Almighty" (El Shaddai), but not as Yahweh. N.B.: Throughout this book "God" and "Yahweh" are used interchangeably to refer to the central Deity of the Old Testament. Where "the LORD" is used, it represents the Hebrew YHWH = Yahweh.

3. Also called the Kenite theory, since Jethro was from the Kenite clan of the Midianites. This theory is discussed fully in H. H. Rowley, *From Moses to Qumran* (London: Lutterworth Press, 1963), Ch. 2. For a criticism of the theory, see Theophile J. Meek, *Hebrew Origins,* rev. ed. (Harper & Brothers, 1950), pp. 94 ff.

4. As an example, the *lex talionis,* "life for life, eye for eye, tooth for tooth" (Ex. 21:23 f.; Lev. 24:20), which is probably earlier even than the time of Moses, represents only one stage in the development of civil legislation and morality.

5. The forms of the Decalogue or "Ten Words" in both Ex. 20:2–17 and Deut. 5:6–21 are expansions and elaborations of the original brief sayings.

6. The Hebrew word here translated "before" may also be rendered "besides" without any essential change in the original meaning of the commandment.

7. Another term that may be used is "monolatry," the worship of only one, and in practical terms, the question of the worship of one god or of many was the real issue in Moses' time.

8. This view will be seen to disagree with the arguments for Mosaic monotheism presented, for example, in William F. Albright's *From the Stone Age to Christianity: Monotheism and the Historical Process,* 2d ed. (The Johns Hopkins Press, 1957), pp. 196–207. But compare Rowley, *From Moses to Qumran,* Ch. 2.

9. See the discussions of this idea below in Chs. VI and VII.

10. The subject of miracles cannot be fully discussed here, but readers should have no trouble with Biblical miracles when they are understood as presented in this discussion. For a brief, well-balanced statement on Old Testament miracles, see H. H. Rowley, *The Faith of Israel* (The Westminster Press, 1957), pp. 57–59.

11. One of the best expositions of this idea is G. Ernest Wright, *God Who Acts* (London: SCM Press, Ltd., 1952).

12. The Hexateuch or "six scrolls" refers to the first six books of the Old Testament, Genesis through Joshua. Scholars have long seen the unity of these six books in the theme of promise and fulfillment, that is,

the promise to Abraham being fulfilled in the conquest of Canaan under Joshua.

13. Hebrew *chesed*, frequently translated "steadfast love" in the RSV, is used of the loyalty and responsibility incumbent upon both parties in the covenant relationship.

14. For a thorough study of this problem, see H. H. Rowley, *From Joseph to Joshua* (London: Oxford University Press, 1950).

15. The amphictyony, a confederation usually of six or twelve tribes owing central loyalty to the same god, is found also among other ancient Mediterranean peoples, especially the early Greek peoples in Greece and Asia Minor.

CHAPTER III. The Lord of Hosts: God and War

1. The last half of the thirteenth century is sufficiently exact for our purposes, since the Old Testament traditions that may indicate an earlier invasion or invasions of Canaan by the Hebrews do not appear to have seriously affected Israel's own historiography at this point.

2. The Song of the Well in Num. 21:17–18 could be from this source also, but the author of Numbers does not so state.

3. In regard to this idea, we must keep in mind the period from which it came, and we must remember that we have no right to impose our concepts of what is pleasing to God upon the viewpoint of ancient Israel.

4. See above, p. 56, n.12. In Joshua there are actually more references to the Mosaic covenant, to the LORD's promises and commandments to Moses, than to the Abrahamic promise. But in one sense, the covenant made through Moses was merely a renewal of the patriarchal covenant, although it certainly contained much that was new as well.

5. For a description of the Ark, see Ex. 25:10–22.

6. Although The Book of Joshua gives the superficial impression that the entire Land of Canaan was conquered by Israelites before the death of Joshua, statements in Joshua itself and the events described in Judges and First Samuel more correctly indicate that gaining control of the entire land was an exceedingly difficult task that continued for at least two centuries.

7. Among these enemies The Book of Judges mentions the Moabites, Canaanites, Midianites, Ammonites, and Philistines.

8. This is the so-called "Deuteronomic" pattern of history. This view of history, found in Joshua, Judges, Samuel, and Kings, as well as in many of the later Prophets, is based largely upon convictions like the one stated in Deut. 4:15–40; cf. ch. 28.

9. This poem is probably the oldest extant example of Hebrew literature, dating as it does to the actual time of the conquest of Canaan.

CHAPTER IV. God and Kingship

1. This statement refers particularly to the antimonarchical material in First Samuel mentioned in the preceding section.

2. On this subject the most important work has been done by Sigmund Mowinckel and Aage Bentzen. See Mowinckel, *The Psalms in Israel's Worship*, tr. by D. R. Ap-Thomas (Oxford: Basil Blackwell & Mott, Ltd., 1962), Vol. I, Ch. 5, and Elmer A. Leslie, *The Psalms* (Abingdon-Cokesbury Press, 1949), pp. 55–130.

3. The passage quoted above from I Chron., ch. 29, although attributed to David, is probably fourth century B.C., but some of the psalms that speak of God's sovereignty may be much earlier than this.

4. As in Jer. 31:27–30 and Ezek., ch. 18. See below, Ch. VI.

5. The so-called "royal psalms" (e.g., Ps. 18, 20, 21, 45, 72) are considered to be prayers offered for or by a king for a specific occasion or as a petition for a specific need.

6. Psalms 47; 68; 93; 96; 97; 98; 99.

7. See the references to such ancient records in I Kings 11:41; 14:19, 29, etc.

8. Note the similar remark attributed to the Queen of Sheba in I Kings 10:9.

CHAPTER V. God in the Early Prophetic View

1. See above, Ch. I. On the literature of Ras Shamra, two good surveys in English are Cyrus H. Gordon, *Ugaritic Literature* (Rome: Pontifical Biblical Institute, 1949), and John Gray, *The Legacy of Canaan*, 2d rev. ed. (Leiden: E. J. Brill, 1965).

2. The Old Testament prophets strongly condemned such syncretism on Israel's part. See the discussion of this problem in succeeding sections of this chapter and in Ch. VI.

3. We shall continue to use the term "Israel" to designate all the Old Testament people of God descended from Jacob-Israel. When the Northern Kingdom of Israel alone is meant, some such term as "Northern Israel" will be employed.

4. While Jezebel seems to have been most responsible for the introduction of Baal worship in Israel, the permissiveness of King Ahab involved him in her guilt, according to the Old Testament writers. See I Kings 16:30–33; 17:17–18.

5. This point will be discussed further in the last section of this chapter, on the "Deuteronomic" understanding of God.

6. Moses may be considered one of the first prophets, since he was in every respect a "spokesman" for God; see Ex. 4:10–17; Num. 11:24 f.; chs. 26 to 30.

7. See above, pp. 65 f.

8. See especially Judg. 2:6 to 3:6; I Kings 11:9–13; cf. Deut., chs. 4; 28.

CHAPTER VI. The Great Prophets Speak for God

1. The other prophets of this period, Nahum, Habakkuk, and Zephaniah, will be mentioned where their ideas are relevant to our discussion.

2. This term is discussed above, pp. 51 f.

3. "Second Isaiah" refers to the unknown author of Isa., chs. 40 to 55. See the first section of Ch. VII, below.

4. Millar Burrows, An Outline of Biblical Theology (The Westminster Press, 1946), pp. 57–58.

5. Amos mentions Syria, Philistia, Phoenicia, Edom, Ammon, and Moab, in addition to Israel and Judah; see chs. 1:3 to 2:3.

6. On the "holiness" of Yahweh, see Ch. VIII, below.

7. The book of Deuteronomy is probably a late seventh-century revision of older laws and traditions, many of which were undoubtedly known to the prophets.

8. Even the institution of the monarchy itself was condemned by Hosea (ch. 10:3–10).

9. Lest it be concluded that the eighth- and seventh-century prophets had nothing positive or hopeful to say about Israelite society, see the discussion below of the prophets' view of the future.

10. Examples of this view may be seen in Num. 16:31–33; Josh. 7:24–25; II Sam. 21:1–9.

11. In Ch. III, above, we discussed the problem of idolatry when Israel first settled in Canaan and during the period of the Judges, and in Ch. V during the time of Elijah and Elisha.

12. Scholars of earlier generations made too much of the antipathy between prophet and priest. Still, there is evidence that the prophets and priests frequently clashed over the nature of true religion and the prerogatives of their respective offices. On the role of the prophet within the priestly cultus, see below in Ch. VIII.

13. In Hosea the knowledge of God is expressed in terms of an intimate personal experience. Knowledge is not merely intellectual; it involves emotion as well. In Hebrew thought the individual is a unified

totality, and as such his life and experiences are whole rather than divided into separate parts.

14. See II Kings 14:4; 15:4; 16:2–4, 10–13; 17:15–17.

15. For another statement of this idea, see B. Davie Napier, *From Faith to Faith* (Harper & Brothers, 1955), p. 157.

16. The oracles predicting Babylonia's downfall are numerous. See Isa., chs. 13; 14:3–23; Jer. 50:1 to 51:58; but, strangely, not in Ezekiel.

17. An unusual apocalyptic interpretation of the final victory of God over his foes in the last days is given in Ezek. 38:1 to 39:21.

18. The definitive study is undoubtedly Sigmund Mowinckel, *He That Cometh*, tr. by G. W. Anderson (Oxford: Basil Blackwell & Mott, Ltd., 1956). See also Helmer Ringgren, *The Messiah in the Old Testament* (Alec R. Allenson, Inc., 1956), and Joseph Klausner, *The Messianic Idea in Israel* (The Macmillan Company, 1955). A helpful brief summary is given by E. Jenni, "Messiah, Jewish," in *The Interpreter's Dictionary of the Bible*, ed. by George A. Buttrick *et al.*, Vol. 4 (Abingdon Press, 1962), pp. 360–365.

CHAPTER VII. God in the Later Prophetic View

1. Some poetic passages in Second Isaiah refer to "Jacob" and "Israel" in the parallel constructions (e.g., chs. 40:27; 41:8, 14; 43:1). In this usage the two names denote the whole people of God descended from Jacob-Israel.

2. See the statement above on p. 99.

3. For an excellent treatment of this mythical theme, see Mircea Eliade, *Cosmos and History: The Myth of the Eternal Return*, tr. by W. R. Trask (Harper & Brothers, 1954).

4. The four major Servant poems are located in chs. 42:1–4; 49:1–6; 50:4–11; 52:13 to 53:12.

5. An eponymous individual or corporate personality could also be seen as representative of the tribe or nation, as in the case of Abraham, Isaac, Jacob-Israel, the kings, etc.

6. Here we begin to use the terms "Judaism" and "Jews," since, technically speaking, "Judaism" refers to the particular set of religious beliefs and practices, based to be sure upon the older Israelite faith, that grew out of the time of Babylonian exile and the centuries immediately thereafter.

7. See the discussion of the cultic prophets below in Ch. VIII.

8. Only chs. 1 to 8 are thought to have originated with Zechariah. Chapters 9 to 14 are mostly poetic oracles, probably from the Greek period of Jewish history (ca. 331–164 B.C.).

9. In the Hebrew Bible, Daniel is listed with the Writings, rather than with the Prophets, because the prophetic canon was apparently closed by about 400 B.C., and since Daniel was not written until well after that time, it could only be included among the later Writings.

CHAPTER VIII. God and the Religion of Israel

1. In the Old Testament it is *qodesh,* a word meaning "holiness," "sacredness," "separateness."

2. In Hebrew there is no single word for sin, but the word most frequently used, both in its verbal and derived noun forms, is *chatah,* "to sin," "err," "miss the mark."

3. The Tabernacle (Ex., ch. 26) was a movable holy place. When God "tabernacles" or "tents" with his people, he manifests his presence among them. During its time the Tabernacle was Israel's most sacred place, as Ex. 40:34–38 indicates.

4. See Gen. 12:7 f.; 13:18; 22:9; 26:25; 33:20; 35:1, 3, 7; Ex. 17:15; 24:4–6.

5. In ancient times most sacred objects, places, persons, etc., were considered *tabu* (a Polynesian word meaning "set apart" or "forbidden"). Such objects could not be touched or violated by someone who was not qualified, by virtue of a like sacredness, to do so.

6. In the next chapter we shall discuss Psalms more fully as representative of the later religious poetry of the Old Testament. Careful studies of the literature of Psalms have revealed many new aspects and details of Israel's worship over several centuries of her history.

7. The Passover sacrifice described in Ex. 12:1–28 is probably a later ritualizing of a primitive nomadic custom whose historical importance is now completely identified with the exodus traditions.

8. Notably Ps. 6; 28; 31; 69; 85.

9. For a survey of this research, see J. Stanley Chesnut, "The Promises of Restoration in the Book of Jeremiah," unpublished Ph.D. dissertation, Yale University, 1959 (University Microfilms, Inc., Ann Arbor, Michigan), pp. 128–138.

CHAPTER IX. God in Wisdom and Poetry

1. Two additional wisdom books, Ecclesiasticus and The Wisdom of Solomon, are included in the Old Testament Apocrypha.

2. Lyric poetry is also found in The Song of Songs (Solomon), which is a collection of secular love songs that tells us nothing about the Old Testament understanding of God. It was included in the Old

Testament canon only after having been allegorized by Jewish commentators who saw in it the love of God for Israel and of Israel for God.

3. For example, "I tell you, that to every one who has will more be given; but from him who has not, even what he has will be taken away" (Luke 19:26).

4. "Ecclesiastes" is the Greek form of the Hebrew word *Qoheleth*, meaning "one who directs a congregation or school." The author assumed the literary role of King Solomon, especially in chs. 1 and 2 (cf. chs. 1:1, 12; 2:4–9), although he does not use the name.

5. For a discussion of specific interpolations, see Julius A. Bewer, *The Literature of the Old Testament,* rev. ed. (Columbia University Press, 1933), pp. 337–339.

6. The present collection was arranged in five "Books" (Ps. 1 to 41; 42 to 72; 73 to 89; 90 to 106; 107 to 150), perhaps to parallel the five books of the Law.

CHAPTER X. God of the Covenant: Old and New

1. It is well known that the word "testament" (from Latin *testamentum,* "witness") when used of the two parts of the Bible has the meaning of "covenant" (from Latin *convenire,* "assembly," "agreement"). Both words are used with reference to the agreements made by God with his people, whether Israel or the church.

2. The Kingdom had been divided into Israel and Judah at the death of Solomon, ca. 935 B.C., but the monarchical system remained in effect. It was considerably more effective in Judah, where loyalty to the Davidic dynasty made possible a more stable situation. Israel was beset with regicide, frequent usurpation of the throne, and thus little dynastic continuity.

3. Jeremiah sometimes refers to all God's people as "Israel," but in most of the oracles of restoration he distinguishes Israel from Judah and includes both in the future hope. See Chesnut, "The Promises of Restoration in the Book of Jeremiah," pp. 65–69.

Index

Aaron, 47, 132, 137
Abraham, 14, 24, 41–43, 48, 56, 58, 60, 63 f., 76, 135, 138, 166 f., 168 f.
Adam, 134, 166
Adultery, 91, 108
Ahab, 86 f., 89, 91 f.
Albright, William F., 52n8
Alt, Albrecht, 43n6
Amos, 76, 83, 99, 103, 106 f., 110 f., 171
Amphictyony, 58
Anderson, G. W., 112n18
Angel of the Lord, 41, 66, 78
Animism, 19, 144
Anthropomorphism, 22, 33–35, 36 f.
Apocalyptic, 69, 128, 146
Apostasy, 67, 88–90, 93, 110
Ark of the Covenant, 48, 64 f., 67, 137
Asherah, 85
Ashtoreth, 65, 85
Assyria, 78, 99 f., 110 f.

Baal, Baalism, 65, 84–88, 92, 108, 117, 132, 170

Babel, Tower of, 33
Babylon, Babylonia, 100, 110 f., 114 f., 120 f., 145, 147
Babylonian: creation story, 31 f.; flood story, 32 f.
Beer-sheba, 135 f.
Bentzen, Aage, 74n2
Bewer, Julius A., 161n5
Bible, 18, 22 f., 54, 56, 93
Biblical: interpretation, 20; thought, 69
"Book of Consolation," 115–117
Book of the Covenant, 29, 54, 57
"Book of the Wars of Yahweh," 59 f.
Bultmann, Rudolf, 22
Burrows, Millar, 38n4, 98, 99n4

Canaan, 47, 52, 57, 59 f., 62, 64 f., 82, 84–86, 101, 136, 167, 169 f.
Canaanites: and Hebrews, 29; religion of, 65 f., 84–86, 132
Charisma, charismatic, 14, 72, 80
Chesed, 57n13, 93, 172
Chesnut, J. Stanley, 143n9, 173n3
Christian faith, 20, 24 f., 124 f., 174

Commandments, 50, 54, 94, 102, 130 f., 134

Community, 57, 76, 104 f., 125, 138, 147, 161 f., 166 f., 168, 171, 174 f.

Conquest of Canaan, 59 f., 63

Corporate personality, 104

Cosmology, 38 f., 119

Covenant: faithfulness, 57, 66 f., 101, 106, 130, 134, 146, 167, 170–172; with Israel, 51, 55–57, 62, 67 f., 73, 96, 120, 165–175; with Moses, 44, 166; with Noah, 33, 56, 166

Covenant Code. See Book of the Covenant

Creation: God and, 35–39; story of, 21, 34, 35–38, 40, 116 f., 122; Wisdom and, 152

Credo, Israelite, 42, 56

Cult, cultus, 47, 96, 106–108, 125–127, 134, 139, 143, 145, 162 f.

Cyrus, 113 f., 120–122, 145

Daniel, 125, 128

Daniel, Book of, 128, 172

David, 45, 61, 64, 73, 76, 78, 91, 112, 136, 140, 169 f.

Day of Atonement, 141

Day of the Lord, 79, 97, 111 f., 126 f.

Decalogue. See Ten Commandments

Demythologizing, 22 f.

Deuteronomic: history, 66n8, 93, 110, 136, 140; school, 100 f., 154; thought, 89n5, 92–94, 105

Deuteronomy, book of, 54, 56, 63, 92 f., 130, 148, 166, 168

E tradition. See Elohist

Ecclesiastes, 16 f., 150 f.

Ecclesiastes, book of, 150 f., 159–161

Eden, Garden of, 35 f.

Egypt, 29, 42, 48, 53, 55, 57–59, 61 f., 70 f., 78, 110 f., 120, 122, 140, 147, 167, 169, 173

El Shaddai, 42, 48 f., 166

Election, 55 f., 68, 73, 166

Eliade, Mircea, 122n3

Elijah, 76, 83, 86–88, 91 f., 101, 117, 170

Elisha, 83, 86–88, 101, 170

Elohist, 42 f., 45 f., 48, 166

Eschatology, 68 f., 79–81, 97, 111 f., 116 f., 124, 172

Ethical monotheism, 50, 99–101, 107

Ethical theme, 33, 68, 96

Etiologies, 37

Evil, evils, 96, 102, 132, 154 f., 172

Evolution, concept of, 18 f.

Exile, Babylonian, 76, 113–117, 120 f., 123 f., 131, 145, 147, 167, 173

Existentialism, 23

Exodus, book of, 44–46, 49, 54–56, 86, 93, 122, 130, 137, 166, 168

Exodus, the, 29, 44 f., 47, 52–54, 59, 62, 64, 93, 116 f., 140

Ezekiel, 69, 92, 105 f., 108, 110 f., 117, 171

Ezra, 130, 146, 172

Faith: covenant, 57, 66 f., 101, 106, 167 f.; of Israel, 14, 18, 43, 46, 52 f., 55, 65, 119

Fear of God, 50, 131–135, 151 f., 160 f.

Flood story, 32 f.

Forgiveness, 109, 127

Genesis, book of, 21, 29 f., 31–33, 34, 35–38, 40, 42, 45, 85, 130, 138, 148

Gilgamesh, 32

God: as anthropomorphic, 22, 33–35, 36 f.; as Being, 16, 34, 35, 50, 90, 104, 160; as compassionate, 53 f., 127; as Creator, 21, 36 f., 49 f., 70, 86, 100, 115, 119 f., 123, 131, 143, 146, 150, 157 f., 161, 166; as holy, 49 f., 79, 116, 131–135; as imminent, 38, 142; as jealous, 50, 66, 88, 130; as King, 70–81, 96, 100, 120, 131, 163, 169; as living, 36, 40, 142 f., 154; as Lord of existence, 36, 49 f., 69, 86; as Lord of history, 49 f., 53, 60, 68, 74, 86, 93, 97, 115, 120, 131, 149, 154, 158, 161; as personal, 40, 50, 85, 142, 154, 160 f., 164; as Redeemer, 120–125, 146, 161; as righteous, 50, 91 f., 132 f., 171; as Ruler, 49, 76–81, 89, 100, 113, 146, 154, 157 f., 160, 169; as transcendent, 50, 143

God: acting in history, 52 f., 64, 66, 97, 100, 109–112, 116, 120 f., 154, 167; and creation, 35–38, 150; and his people, 20, 70, 101 f., 108 f., 133, 145, 156–158; and nature, 38 f., 49 f., 69, 96; and the social order, 101–104; and war, 59–69, 169; and wisdom, 147–165; breath of, 36, 40; existence of, 14 f., 160; fear of, 50, 131–135, 151 f., 160 f.; knowledge of, 15–17, 107n13, 160, 173; of the covenant, 165–175; of the Fathers, 41–43, 55; revealed in history, 18, 68, 83 f., 111; the Spirit of, 36, 39–41, 66, 72, 79, 83, 87, 127, 152; worship of, 141–144, 160 f.

Gods, 31, 42, 51, 65–67, 88, 100, 109, 117–120, 128, 130, 166

Gordon, Cyrus H., 85n1

Gray, John, 85n1

Greek thought, 51, 151 f., 159

Haggai, 125 f., 171

Hammurabi, Code of, 29, 54

Hanukkah, Feast of, 141

Harlotry, 108 f., 117

Hebrew, Hebrews, 26, 28, 31, 44, 98, 104, 150, 159

Henotheism, 50 f., 95

Hexateuch, 56, 64, 169

History: interpretation of, 46, 64, 116 f., 156, 167; meaning of, 22 f., 71, 77; of religion, 18, 129 f., pattern of, 65 f., 66n8; prophetic view of, 19, 71; sacred, 53

Historical revelation, 17–19

Holiness, 97, 131–135, 139

Holiness Code, 133–135

Holy One, 100, 110, 116, 122, 131–133, 135, 137, 142, 161

Holy war, 62–65

Horeb, 46 f.

Hosea, 99, 107–109, 110 f., 171 f.

Idolatry, idols, 92, 96, 99, 106, 109, 114, 117–119, 130, 137, 170 f.

Immorality, 96, 103 f., 110

Individual responsibility, 105–106

Individualism, 76 f., 104–106

Ingathering, Feast of, 141

Isaac, 24, 41–43, 48, 135

Isaiah, 76, 92, 99 f., 103, 108 f., 110, 113 f., 132, 171

Isaiah, The Book of, 113 f.

Israel, 41, 57 f., 62, 100, 108, 110 f., 112, 123 f., 130, 133 f., 167, 169, 172 f.

J tradition. *See* Yahwist

Jacob, 24, 41–43, 48, 76, 135 f.

Jenni, E., 112n18

Jeremiah, 92, 105–108, 110 f., 123, 171–174

Jericho, 61, 64

Jerusalem, 78, 100, 103, 105, 107, 110, 113, 117, 120–122, 125–127, 136 f., 171

Jesus, 24, 39, 75, 124, 158, 174

Jesus Christ, 24

Jethro, 47, 138

Jews, 120 f., 125, 128, 136, 141, 145, 158, 161, 171 f., 174

Jezebel, 86 f., 89, 91 f.

Job, 14, 16, 20, 154–158, 160

Job, Book of, 16, 150, 153, 155–158, 160

Joel, 125, 171

Jonah, 20, 125, 127, 172

Joshua, 59, 61, 67, 92, 126, 167

Joshua, Book of, 60, 63 f., 149 f., 172

Josiah, 136, 172

Judah, 99, 105, 110 f., 115, 127, 167, 169, 171, 173

Judaism, 24, 125, 130, 141, 144–146, 147, 153, 155, 167, 174

Judges, 103, 167

Judges, Book of, 60, 64–66, 92 f., 130, 148

Judges, days of the, 65–67, 169 f.

Judgment, 54, 67–69, 79, 99, 102, 109 f., 114 f., 123, 126 f., 170

Judgment Day, 69, 97, 111

Just retribution, 153–155, 167

Justice, 50, 68, 80, 103, 106, 154–158

Kingdom of God, 73–75, 79–81

Kingdom of Israel, 74, 86, 170, 173

Kingdom of Judah, 74, 86, 170, 173

Kings, books of, 77, 92, 130

Kings of Israel, 71, 76 f., 102 f., 140, 163, 167

Kingship, 70–74, 169 f.

Klausner, Joseph, 112n18

Knowledge of God, 15–17, 107n13

Kramer, Samuel Noah, 32n3

Language: of Old Testament, 20–22, 142 f.; religious, 21, 34, 53; symbolic use of, 23

Law, 57, 128, 131, 134, 145 f., 167–169, 172 f.

Leslie, Elmer A., 74n2

Leviticus, book of, 130, 133 f., 137–139, 168

Lex talionis, 50n

Life, 36, 40, 152 f., 158, 159–161

Literary criticism, 21, 27, 28n1
Lord of Hosts, 61 f., 100

Malachi, 126 f., 171
Man: creation of, 40; nature of, 32, 134; relation with God, 156–158, 173 f.
Mesopotamia: land of, 19, 29, 30–33, 35 f., 70; myths from, 27, 90, 141
Messiah, 71 f., 79 f., 97, 112, 124, 126, 146
Micah, 100, 102 f., 107, 110, 171
Monarchy, 73, 78, 170
Monotheism, 19, 51 f., 88, 95 f., 98–101, 114, 117, 119–121, 144, 146, 162
Moses, 14, 20, 28 f., 42 f., 44–58, 59, 60–63, 76, 90, 106, 119, 132, 138, 141, 167 f., 172
Mt. Sinai, 44, 46 f., 136
Mowinckel, Sigmund, 74n2, 112n18
Mythology, 21 f., 38, 85

Near East, 19, 28, 30–33, 37, 39, 70, 80, 120
New Covenant, 171–175
New Testament, 22 f., 24 f., 39, 54, 70, 106, 126, 158, 165
New Year, 74, 77, 141, 163
Noah, 33, 35, 56, 166
Northern Kingdom (Israel), 86, 89, 99 f., 103, 107, 110, 115, 135, 170
Numbers, book of, 59 f., 130

Obedience, 91, 96, 130 f., 133, 135, 144, 151
Old Covenant, 165–172

P (Priestly) tradition, 35, 40, 45, 48, 131, 134, 138 f., 145, 168
Patriarchal traditions, 41–43
Patriarchs, 35, 41–43, 85, 104, 138, 165
Pentateuch, 27, 29, 34, 45n1, 166
People of God, 20, 70, 101 f., 108 f., 115
Persia, 113 f., 120, 125, 127, 141
Poetry, Old Testament, 147 f., 161–164
Polytheism, 18, 21, 43, 130, 144
Prayer, 137, 161 ff.
Priests, 63, 103, 126, 138–140, 142, 145
Primitive religion, 39, 43, 131–133, 138 f., 144
Promised Land, 63–65, 122, 168
Promises, divine, 24, 166 ff.
Prophecy, Hebrew, 82–86, 95–98
Prophets: and predictions, 93, 111 f.; and priests, 107n12, 125–127, 131, 143; as spokesmen, 15 f., 55, 83 f.; court, 84, 103; cultic, 84, 125, 140, 143; knowledge of God, 15 f.; post-exilic, 114, 125–128; sons of the, 84, 87; view of history, 19 f., 69, 71, 92–94, 109–112
Proverbs, book of, 16, 148, 150–153, 156
Psalms, 16, 61, 71, 77, 119, 130, 138, 148 f., 161–164
Punishment, 67–69, 79, 114, 126, 145, 153–155, 170 f.

Qodesh, 131n1

Redemption, 113 f., 121–125, 167, 174

Religion of Israel, 17, 45, 52, 90, 96, 106 f., 129–148, 167 f., 170 f.

Restoration, 111 f., 114–117, 121, 145, 171 f.

Revelation, 17, 82–84, 128, 152

Rowley, H. H., 47n3, 52n8, 53n10, 58n14

Sabaoth, 60–62

Sabbath, 32, 96, 130, 141

Sacred: actions, 129, 136–138; objects, 129, 136 f.; persons, 129, 139 f.; places, 129, 135 f.; times, 129 f., 140 f.

Sacrifice, 47 f., 63, 91, 96, 107, 124 f., 137–139, 145, 168

Sages, 16, 131, 147 f., 156, 159, 167

Samaria, 99, 103, 110

Samuel, books of, 72, 90, 92, 130, 148–150

Saul, 73, 83, 91, 112, 140, 170

Second Isaiah, 19, 52, 98, 104, 113–125, 127, 145, 149 f., 159, 171

Sin, sins, 99, 104, 134, 157, 171

Sinai, 14, 42, 54 f., 56 f., 168

Solomon, 45, 78, 96, 136, 147, 161, 170

Sovereignty of God, 71, 73 f., 78, 79 f., 87, 95 f., 128

Spirit of God, 36, 39–41, 67, 72, 80, 83, 87, 127, 152

Suffering, 156–158

Suffering Servant, 114, 120, 122–125, 145, 171

Syncretism, 31, 43, 88–90

Tabernacle, 136–138

Temple, 52, 84, 96, 107–109, 125 f., 131 f., 136–138, 141, 143, 145, 162 f.

Ten Commandments, 50 f., 54, 130

Theocracy, 72–74

Theodicy, 155–158

Theology: and history of religion, 18; early Hebrew, 33 f.; Old Testament, 17 f., 94, 125

Theophany, 54 f., 135 f., 168

Universalism, 79–81, 114, 120, 123 f., 127

Unknown Prophet, 113–125

Wisdom Literature, 16, 104, 119, 146, 147–164

Worship, 96, 125 f., 130–135, 137 f., 141–144, 162–164

Wright, G. Ernest, 53n11

Yahweh: and creation, 32, 49; and the flood, 32 f.; as God of Israel, 45, 48, 70, 133, 166; as God of war, 59 f.; ethical nature of, 90–92, 99–101, 132 f.; identified with God of Fathers, 41–43, 48, 55, 166; known by Moses, 42, 45; religion of, 46–49, 52, 138

Zechariah, 125 f., 171

Zion, 120, 122